Sheffield is a city of many moods: different areas possess different atmospheres. The old industrial heart of the city in the Kelham Island area is quite different in feel from the business quarter around Paradise Square, which is itself worlds apart from the bustle of Fargate.

And so it was in the 19th century. Sheffield was very much a town of contrasts where artists could record those scenes which appealed to them for a variety of reasons.

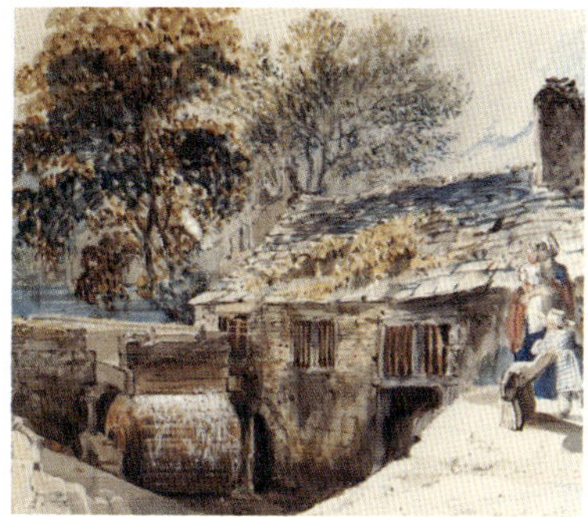

H.P. *Parker*
*Heeley Tilt Forge c.*1840

RURAL *Views*

In 1791, David Martin's drawing of Sheffield from Broomhall Spring was published as part of a group of **Views in the Vicinity of Sheffield.** It shows a small town nestling among hills covered in a patchwork of fields, with the spire of the Parish Church and the lantern tower of St. Paul's Church sticking up above the rooftops. This is Sheffield in its rural setting, at a time before factory chimneys and a great cloud of smoke came to dominate and obscure the

D. Martin
Sheffield from Broomhall Spring 1791

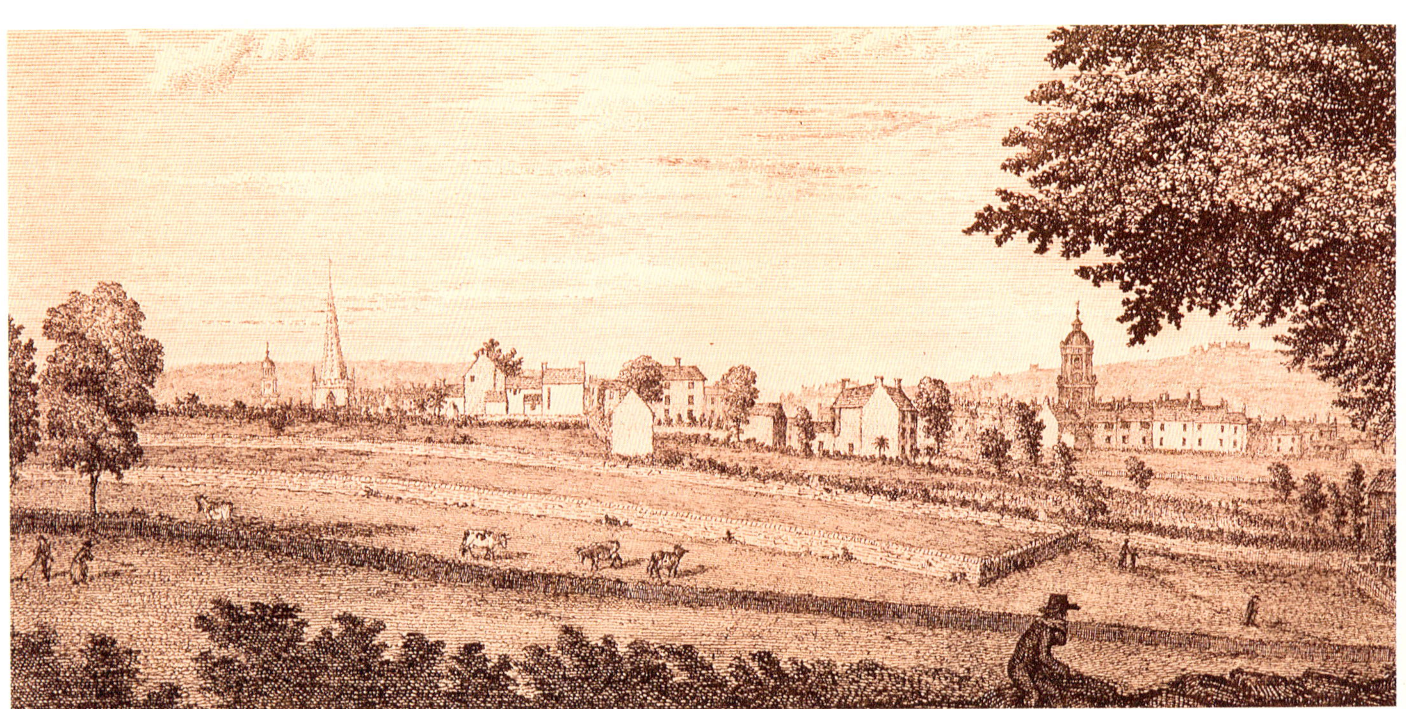

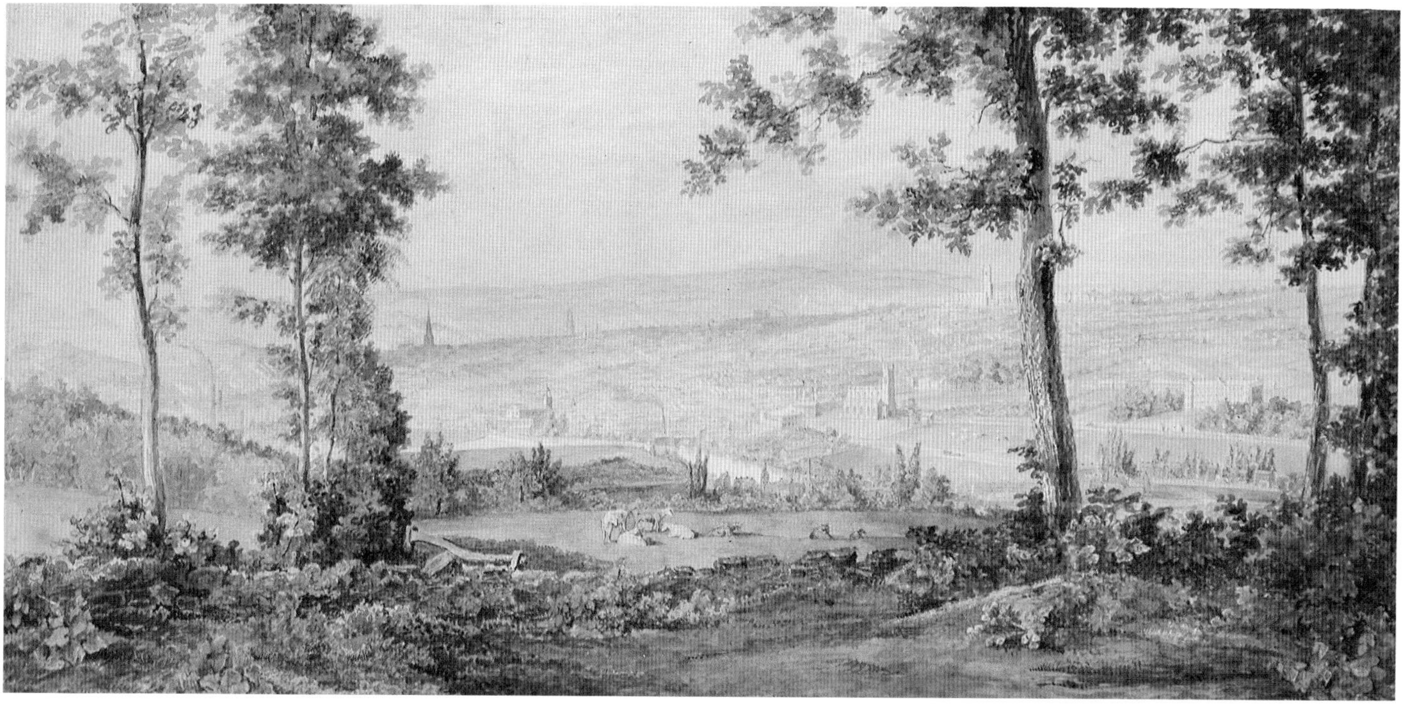

W. *Ibbitt*
*North West view of Sheffield from Parkwood Spring c.*1850

scene. By the 1850s the scale of Sheffield's industrial output had grown enormously but it was still possible — from a further distance — to capture something of the pastoral situation of the rapidly expanding town.

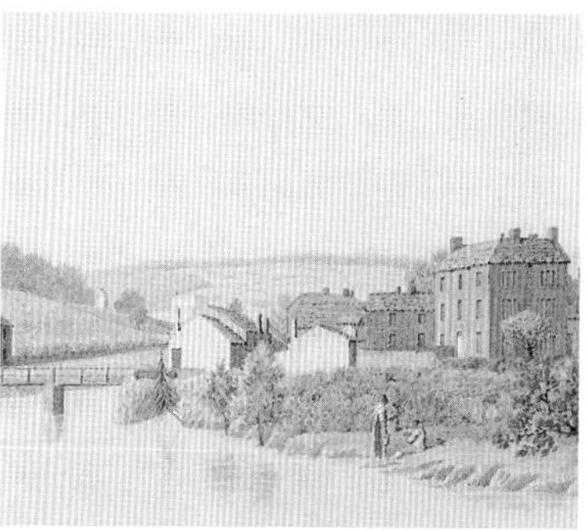

W. *Botham*
Iron Bridge, Sheffield 1802

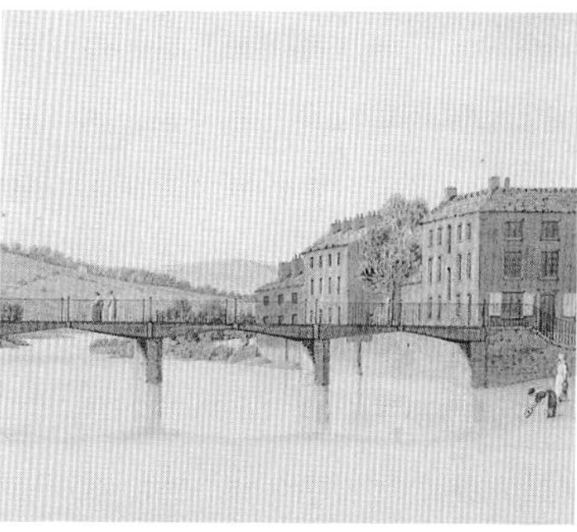

W. *Botham*
Hillfoot Bridge, Sheffield 1802

COUNTRY *Town*

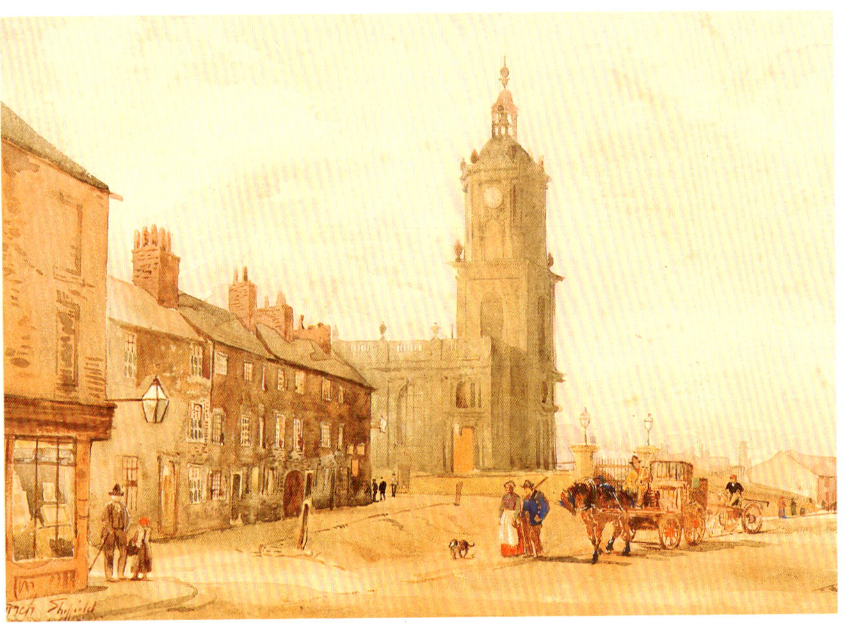

W. Keeling
St. Paul's Church, Sheffield 1885

Throughout the 19th century, and despite all the developments which took place, Sheffield remained essentially a country town, where horses and carts pulling produce to the markets rubbed shoulders with pack horses and carriers taking finished cutlery products away. Keeling's view of St Paul's Church shows such a scene in the 1880s. The view of the Old Cutlers Inn in Fargate and the Iris Office in Hartshead capture the flavour of an easy going way of life whilst Moorhead, for all the advertisements and the railing around the Crimean Monument, still gives the impression of a sleepy place where nothing much ever happens except on market day.

W. Hughes
Hall in the Ponds (Old Queens Head) 1821

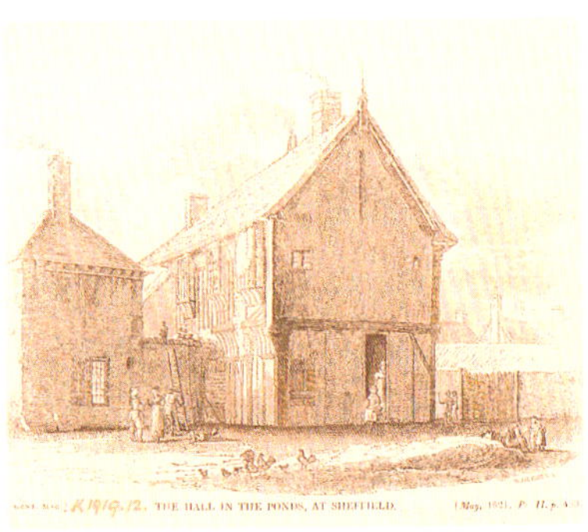

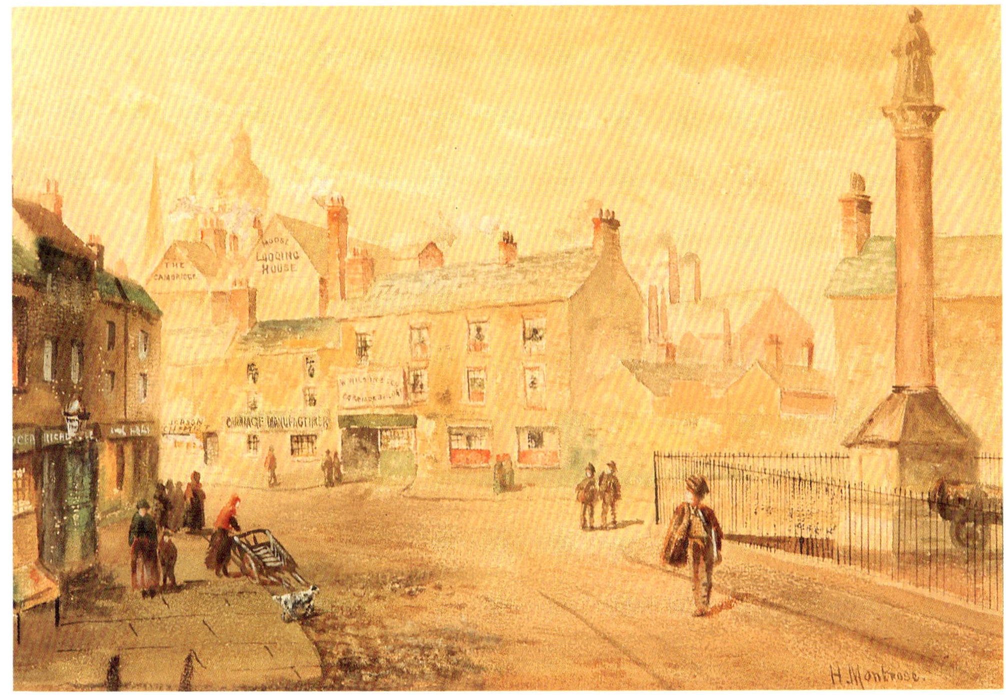

H. Montrose
Old Moorhead c.1860

Anonymous
Cutlers' Inn, Fargate c.1830

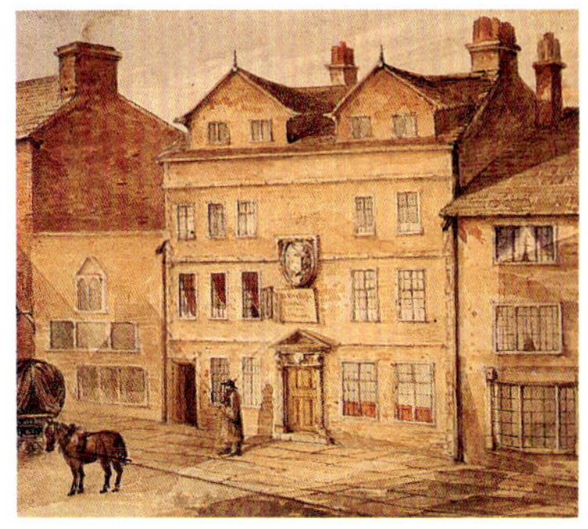

T.P. Willcox
Tontine Hotel, Sheffield c.1830

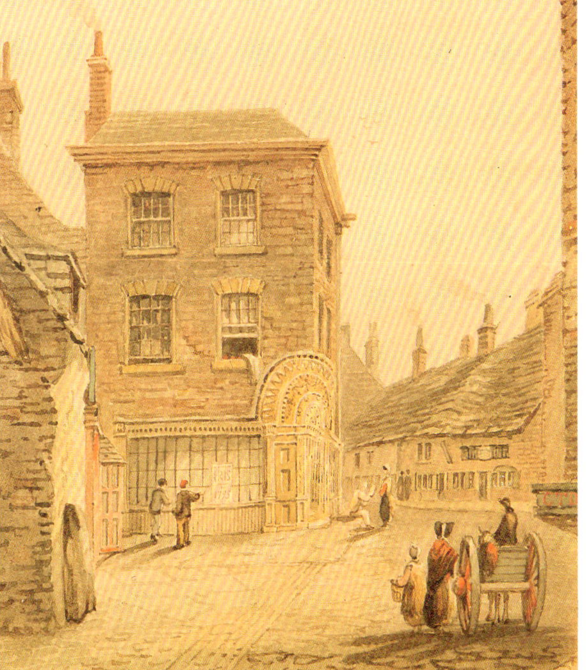

C. Dixon
Iris Office c.1840

W. Botham
Little Hill at the top of Campo Lane 1802

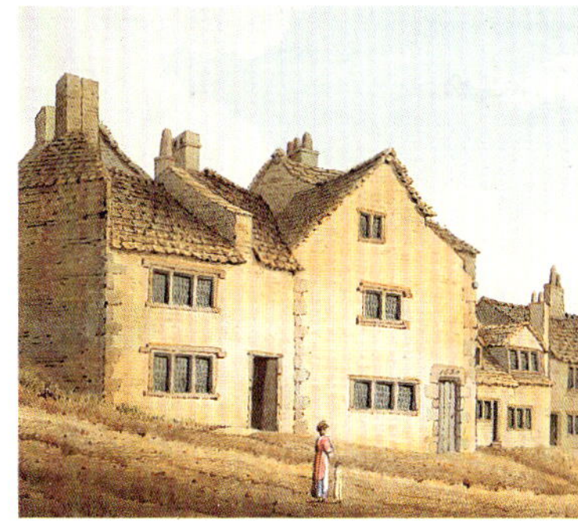

INDUSTRIAL *Town*

Down by the rivers the scene was quite different. An anonymous painting of about 1825 shows Sheaf Bridge, which spanned the River Sheaf at the bottom of Dixon

Anonymous
River Sheaf and Shrewsbury Hospital c.1825

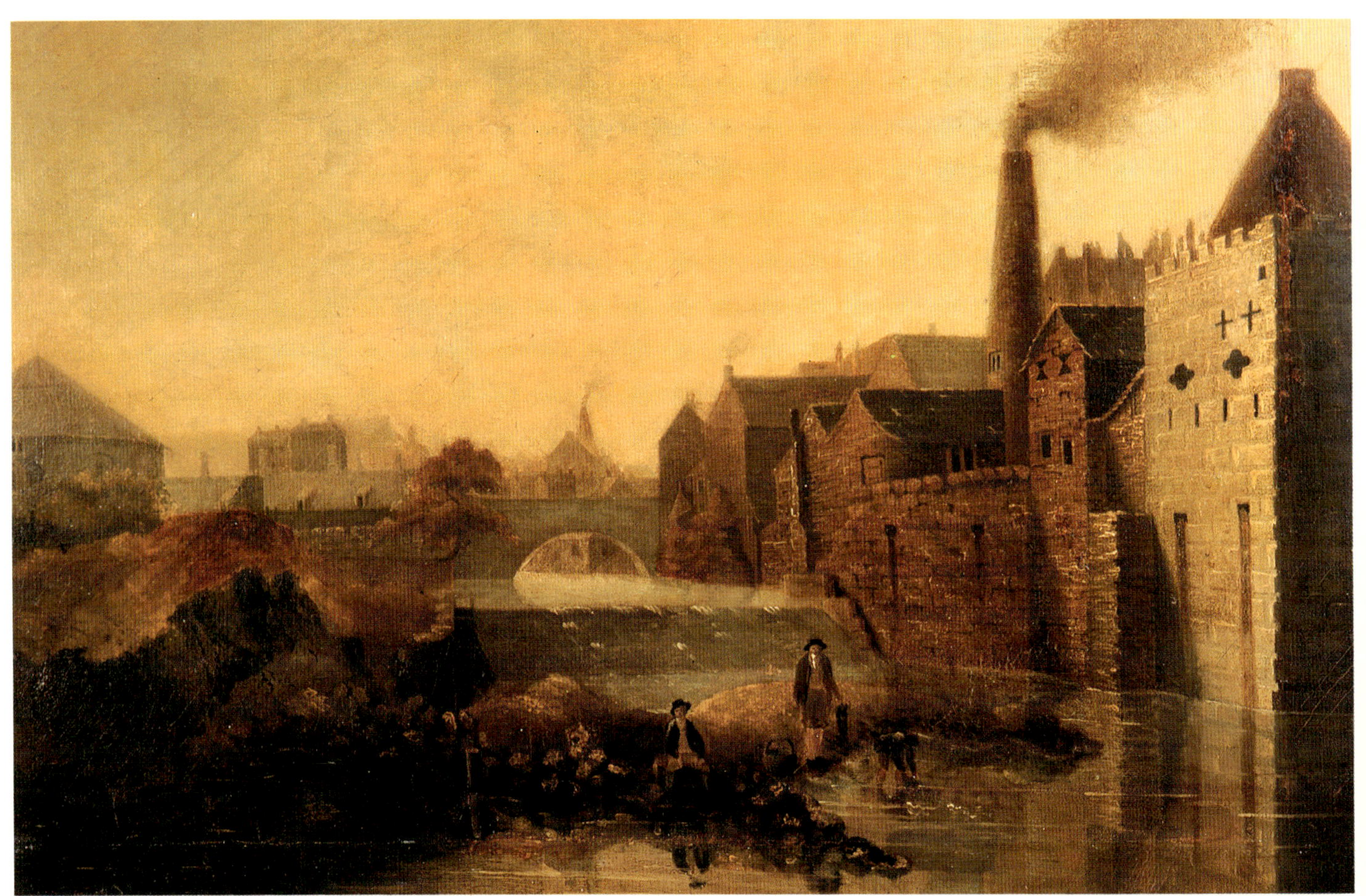

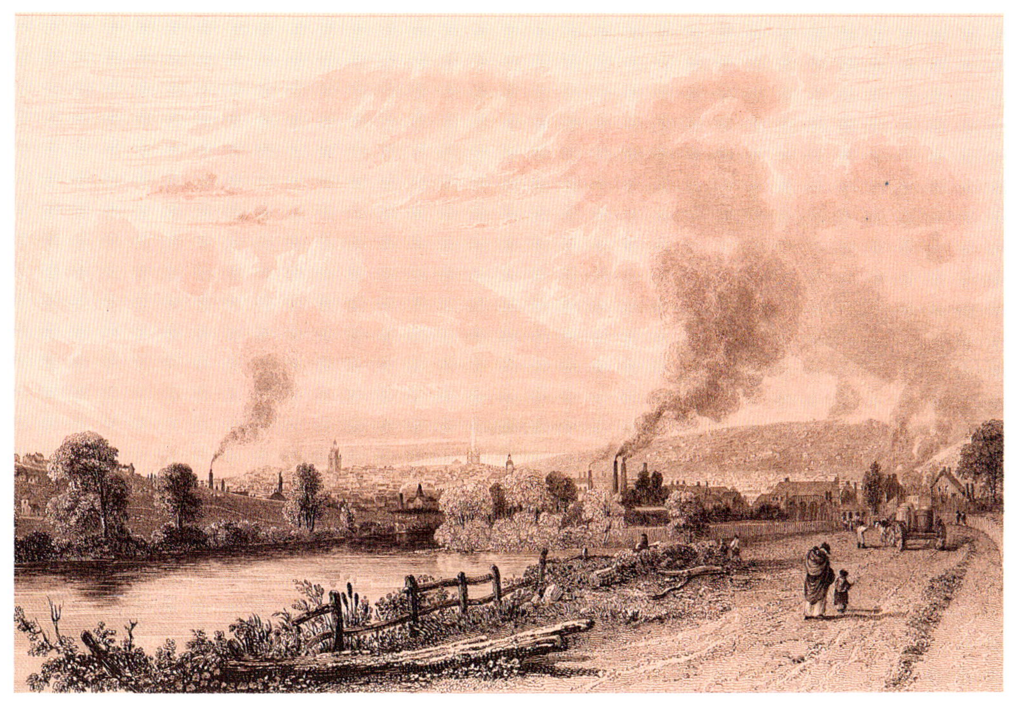

E. Blore
Sheffield from the Attercliffe Road 1819

Anonymous
Bridge and White Rails at Bridgehouses c.1830

Lane, and the conical roof of the Shrewsbury Hospital, the site of which is now buried beneath the Parkway roundabout. On the right hand side the bottle-shaped cementation furnace, factory chimneys and soot-blackened castellated walls declare that this is industrial Sheffield. Further along the River Don, the scene from Bridgehouses is one of smoky chimneys and workshops stretching from the river up the hillside to St George's Church. But the semi-rural character is still apparent in the green fields bordering the river, the donkeys, and chicken huts.

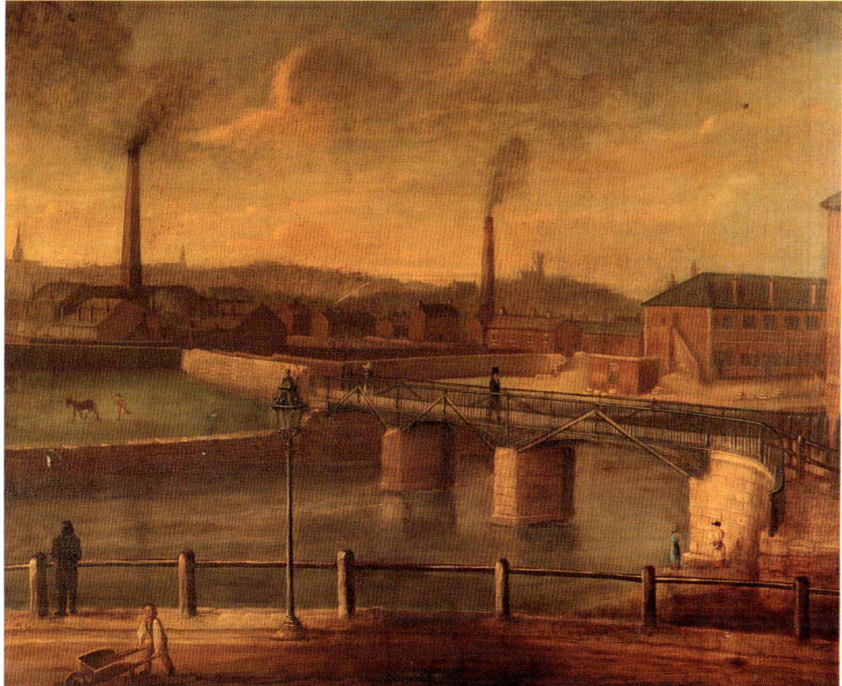

SHEFFIELD
Landscape

Edward Blore's engraving of **Sheffield from Attercliffe Road,** published in 1819, skillfully captures the scene of chimneys and plumes of smoke rising in the distance from the trees and pastures alongside the river. And it was just this image of an industrial town in a country setting which was commented upon in **The Mirror** in 1826:

"Sheffield, in the West Riding of Yorkshire ... is beautifully situated on an eminence at the confluence of the Rivers Sheaf and Don ... and few places can boast of more handsome and regular streets. It is surrounded by hills of considerable height, which command fine prospects of the town and vicinity, and add greatly to the romantic situation of the place. Though the smoke of the manufactories tends to give a sombre appearance, yet the town is far from being dull, and is well furnished as well with the elegancies as the conveniences of life."

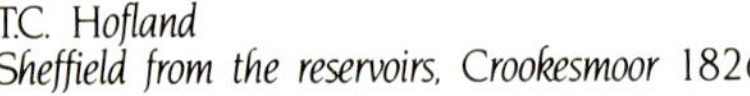
T.C. *Hofland*
Sheffield from the reservoirs, Crookesmoor 1826

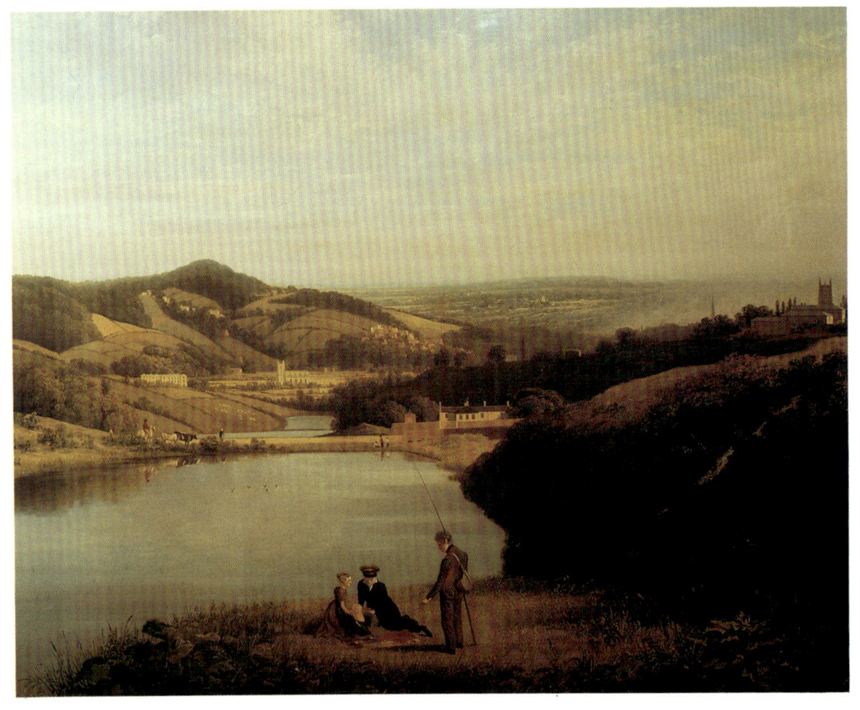

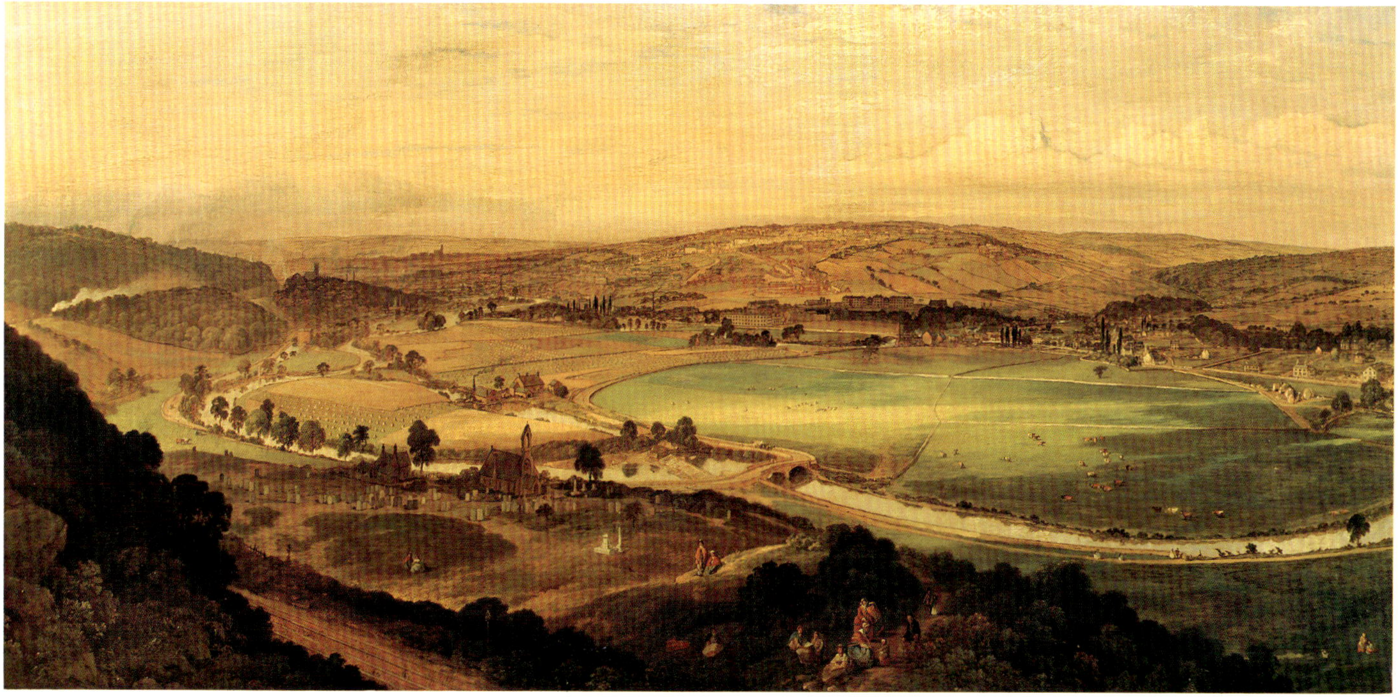

E. Price
Sheffield and the Valley of the Don 1863

J. McIntyre
Sheffield from Psalter Lane, Brincliffe Edge

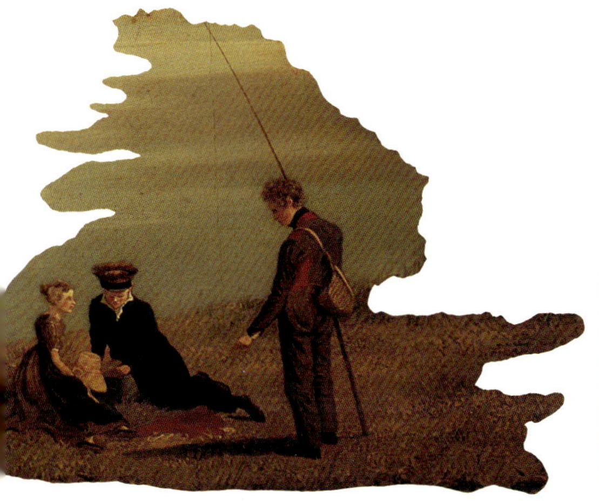

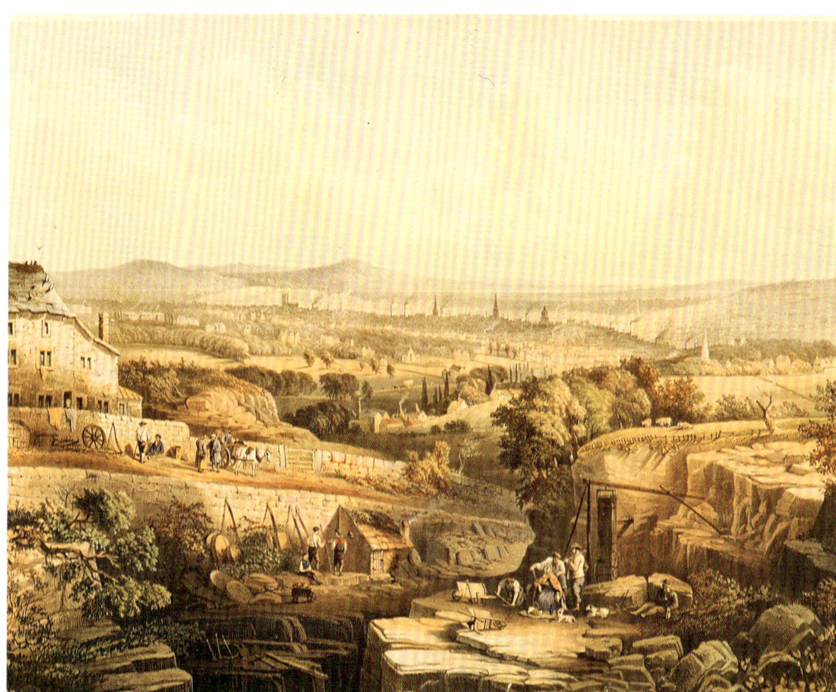

SHEFFIELD *Panorama*

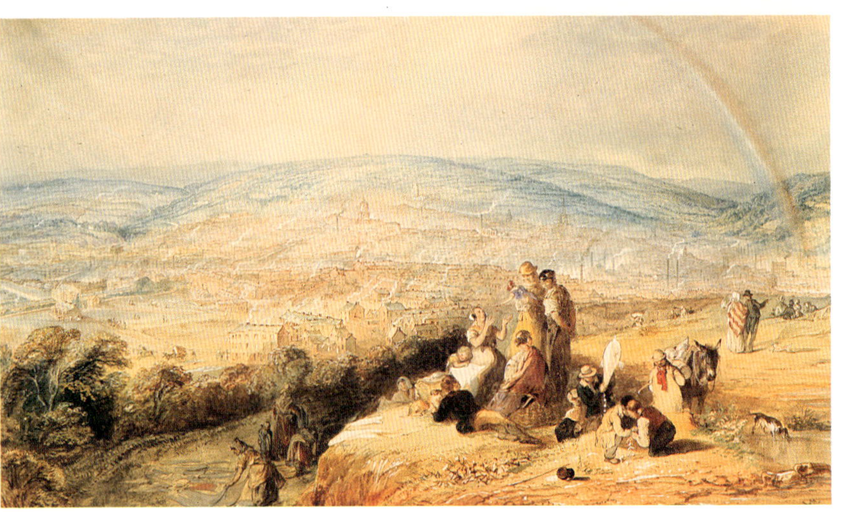

H.P. *Parker*
View of Sheffield from the South East 1843

Sheffield was, indeed, special and throughout the 19th century landscape artists came to capture its unique picturesque quality. Their landscapes and panoramic views also trace the development of the town. William Cowen's **Sheffield from Shrewsbury Road** (1838) is a remarkable townscape contrasting the regular grid-pattern streets of Georgian Sheffield with a rustic foreground scene of horse-drawn vehicles and market girls. H.P. Parker's **South East View of Sheffield** (1843) from Sky Edge shows women laying out washing to dry and boys making kites, whilst behind them the whole prospect of Sheffield with its chimneys is revealed beneath the rainbow. Most marked, however, is the comparison of two views by Wiliam Ibbitt drawn in 1826 and 1854 from virtually the same standpoint. In a space of thirty years the railways have come, industry has grown and the town centre has developed apace.

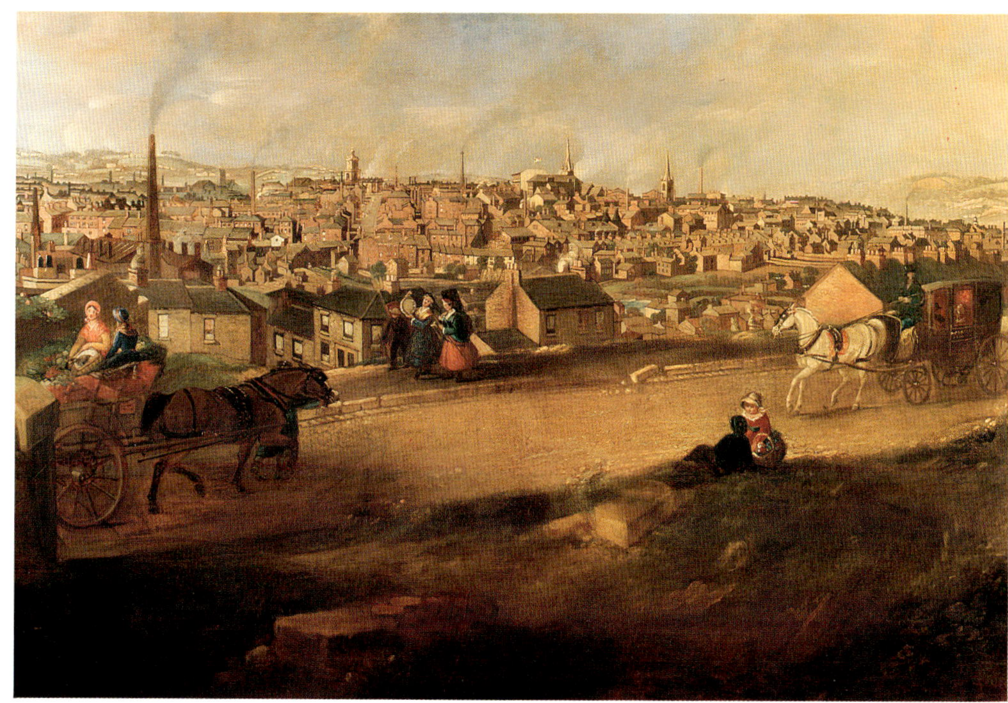

W. Cowen
Sheffield from Shrewsbury Road 1838

W. Ibbitt
South East view of Sheffield 1854

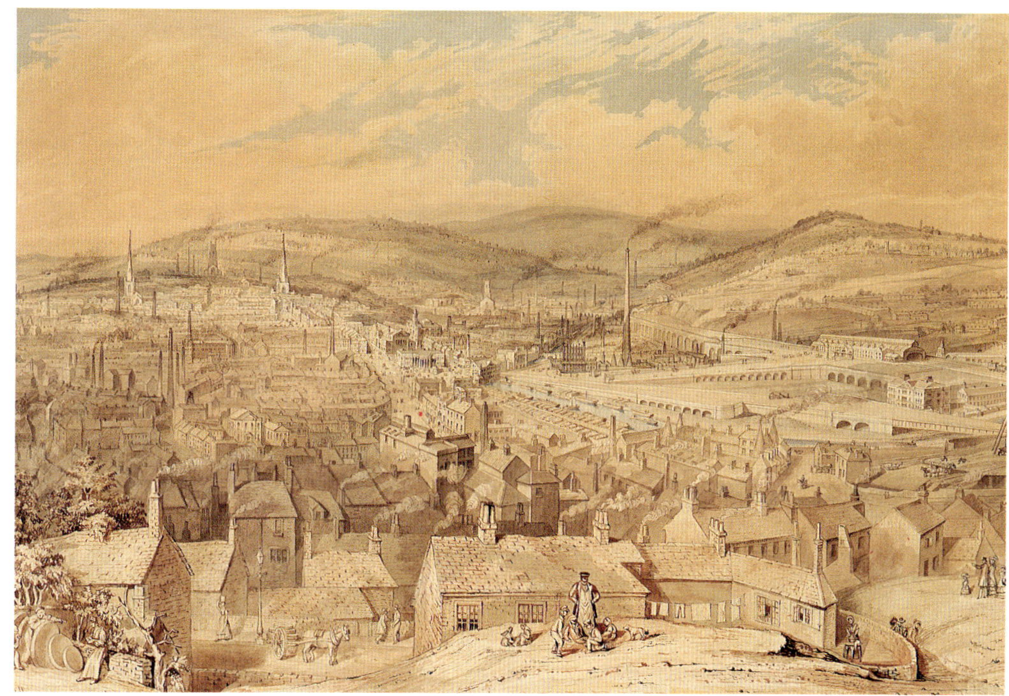

W. Ibbitt
East view of Sheffield 1826

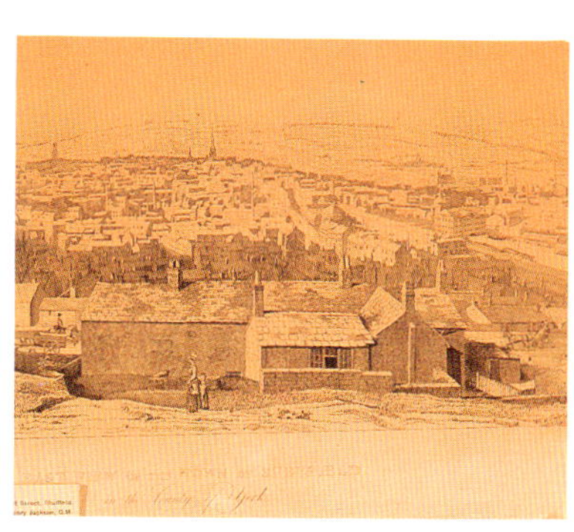

SHEFFIELD *Markets*

Prominent in Ibbitt's town centre scene is the Norfolk Market Hall, built on the site of the Tontine Inn in 1851. Godfrey Sykes, whose paintings constitute a superb record of Sheffield life, painted a picture of this shortly after it was built, and also a picture of the Fitzalan Market Hall further up the High Street, with the statue of Ebenezer Elliott, the Corn Laws poet, in Market Place. Both paintings are teeming with life, as people bustle about their errands or stop to greet one another and exchange news.

G. *Sykes*
Norfolk Market 1853

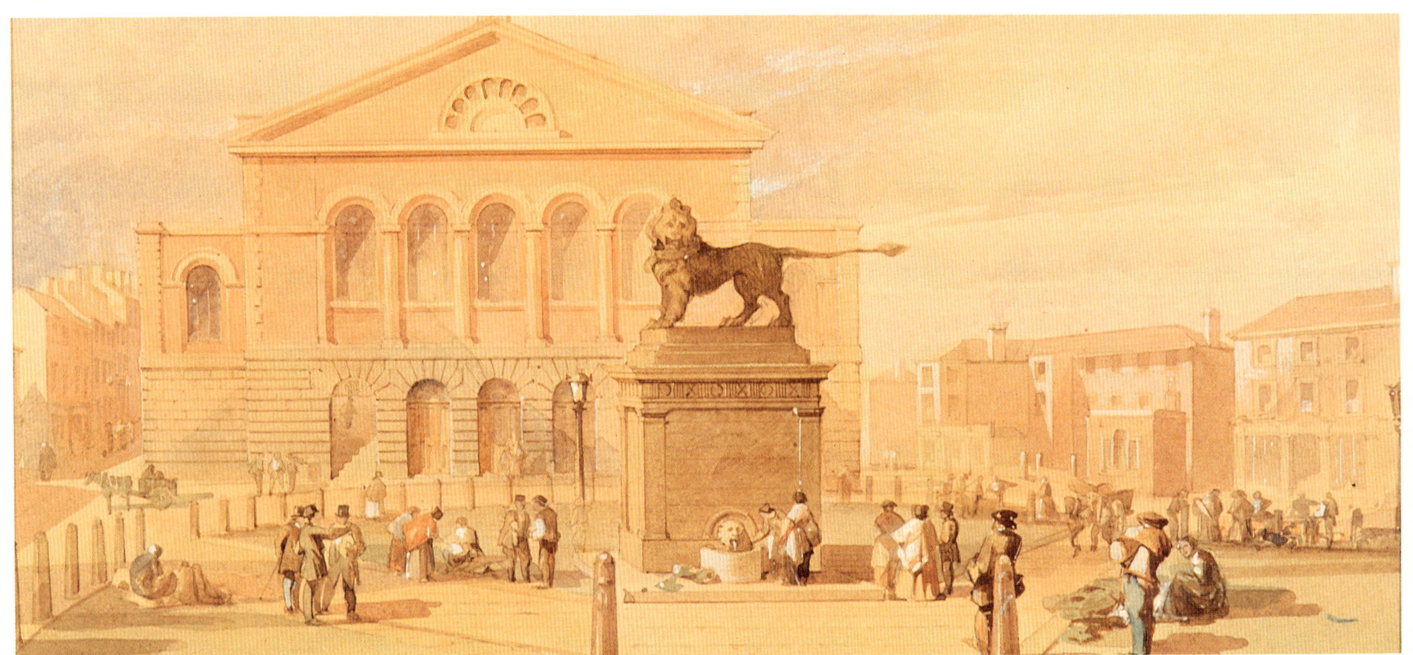

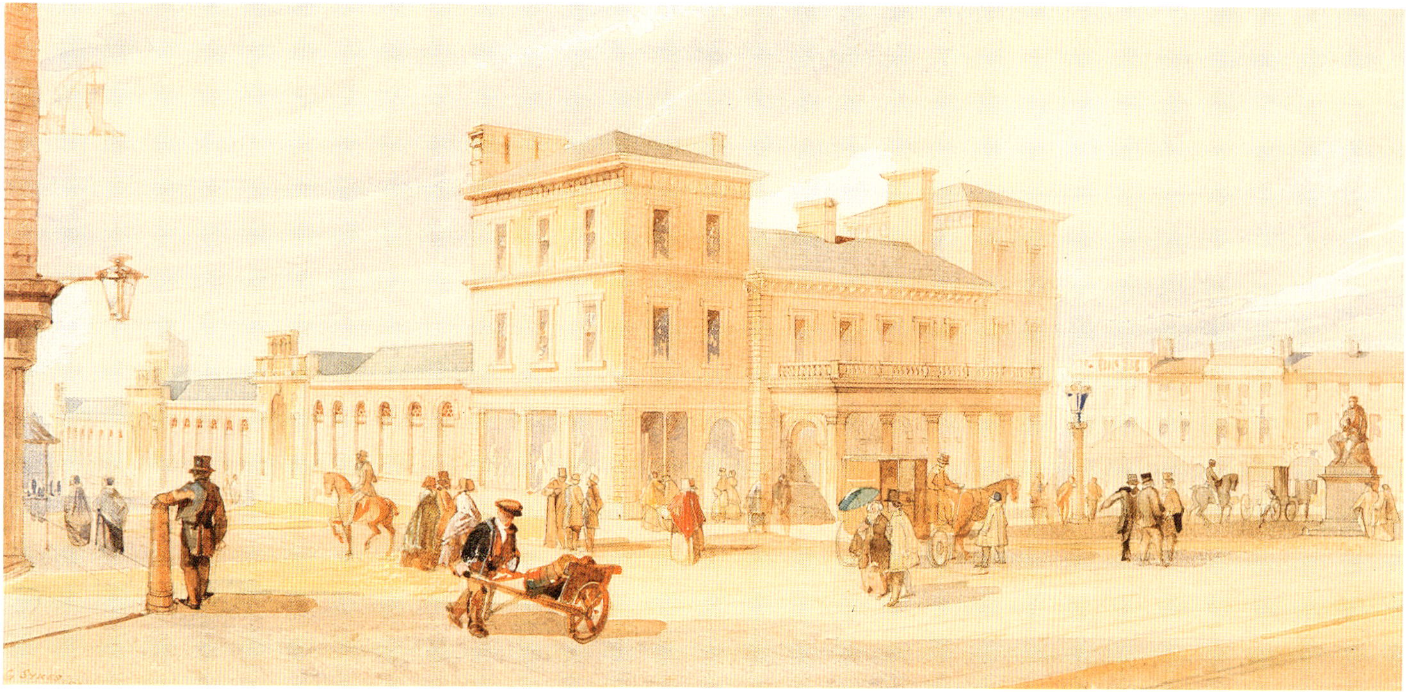

G. Sykes
Fitzalan Market 1853

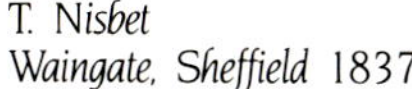

T. Nisbet
Waingate, Sheffield 1837

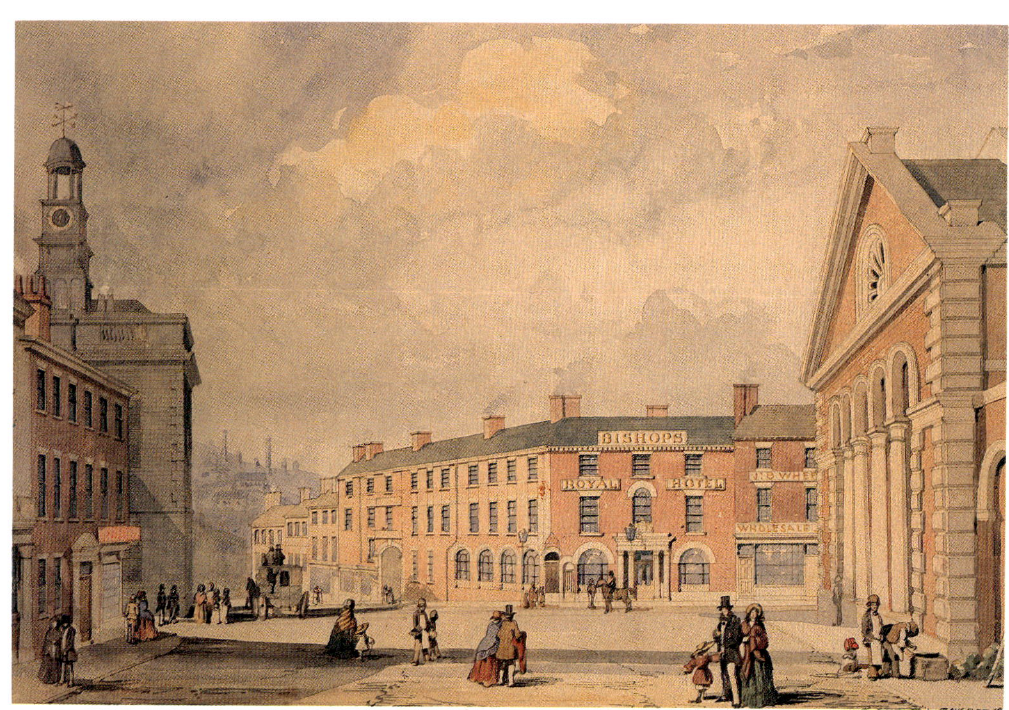

COMMERCIAL *Life*

Sheffield could be a very busy place. Whittock's view of the Town Hall shows a chaotic street scene, whilst Coles Corner at the junction of Fargate and Church Street is as thronged with hurrying people and vehicles as today. The world of shops, commerce, banking, post offices and transport, then as now, equalled noise, speed, quick wits, hassle, smells and weariness. Fortunately, it was not all like that.

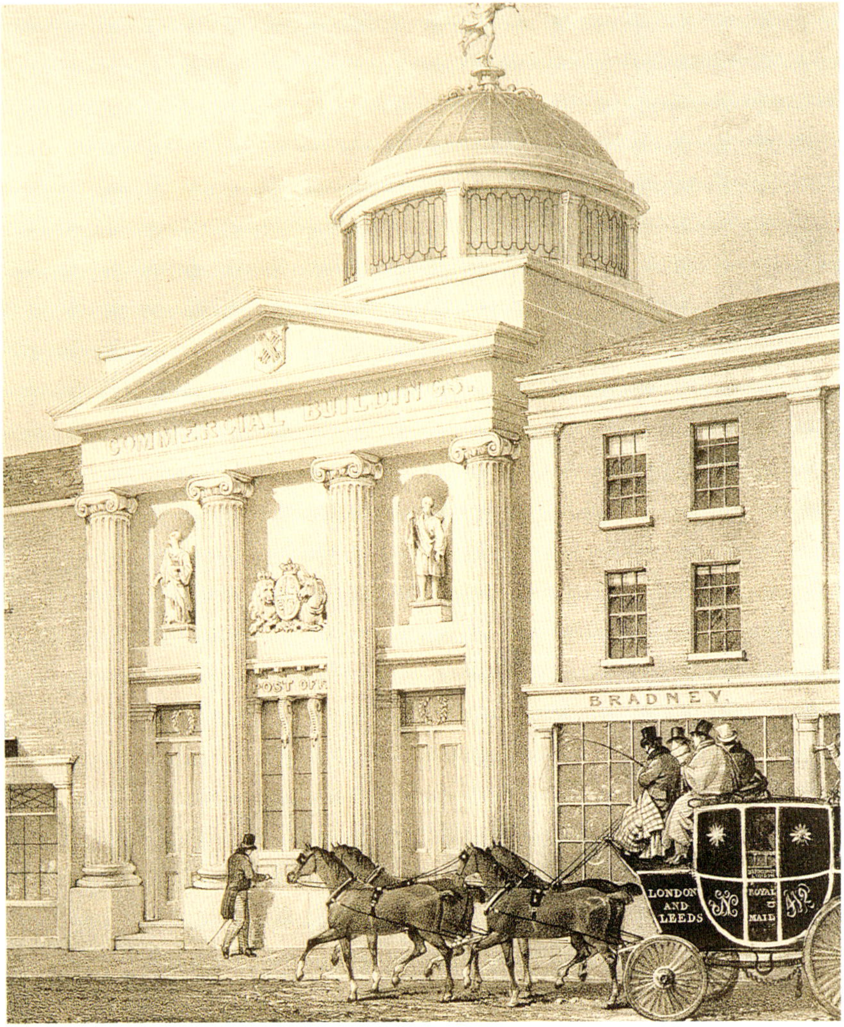

Anonymous
New Club House c.1850

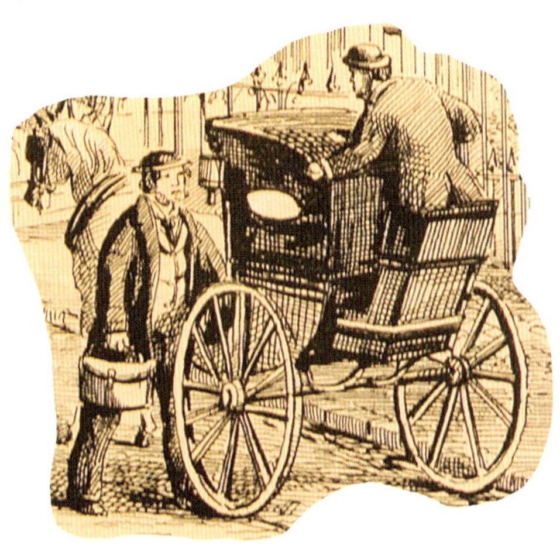

L. Haghe
Commercial Buildings and Post Office c.1840

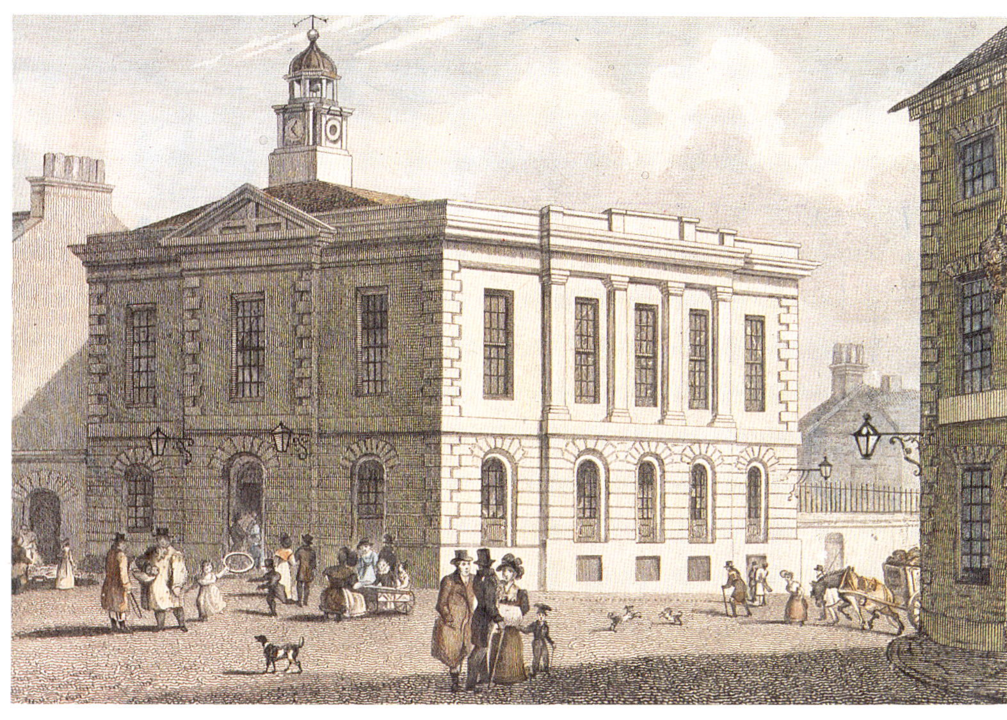

N. Whittock
Town Hall c.1830

Pawson & Brailsford
Coles Corner, Fargate c.1880

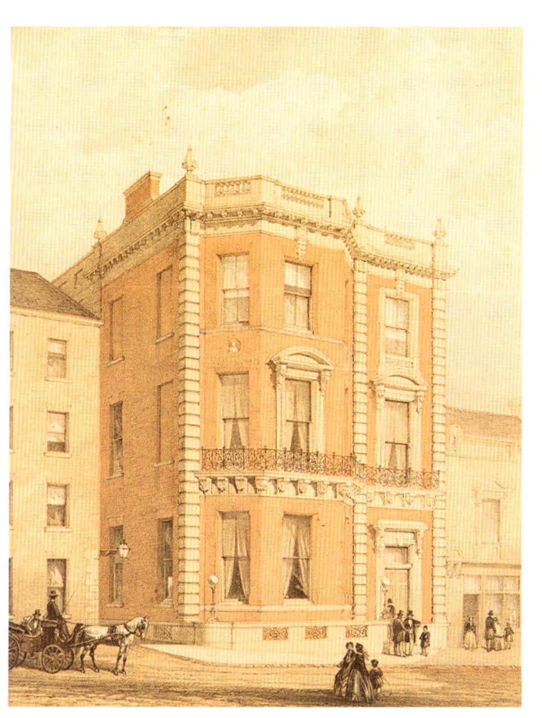

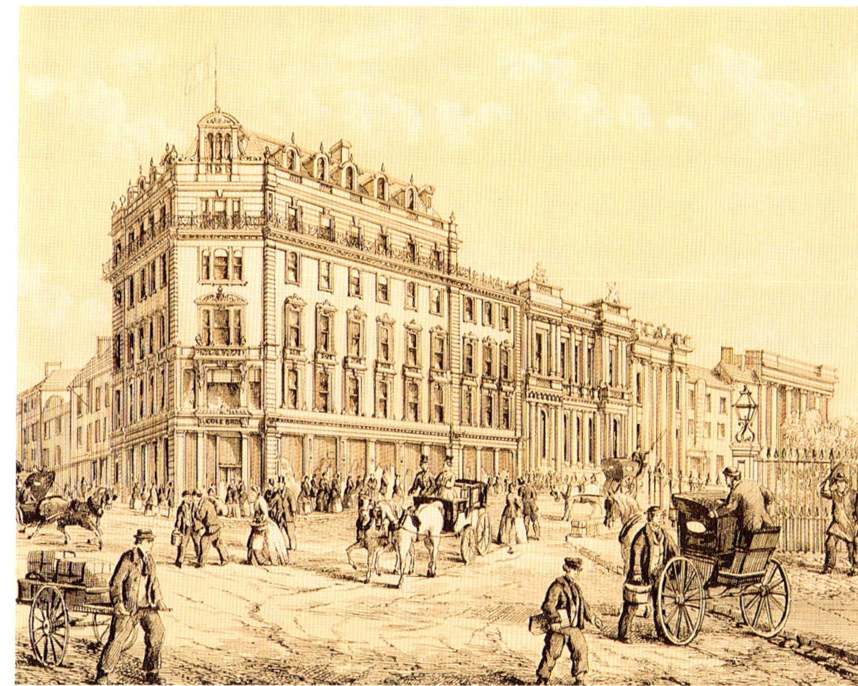

QUIET *Corners*

G. Sykes
Cheney Square with St. Paul's Church 1858

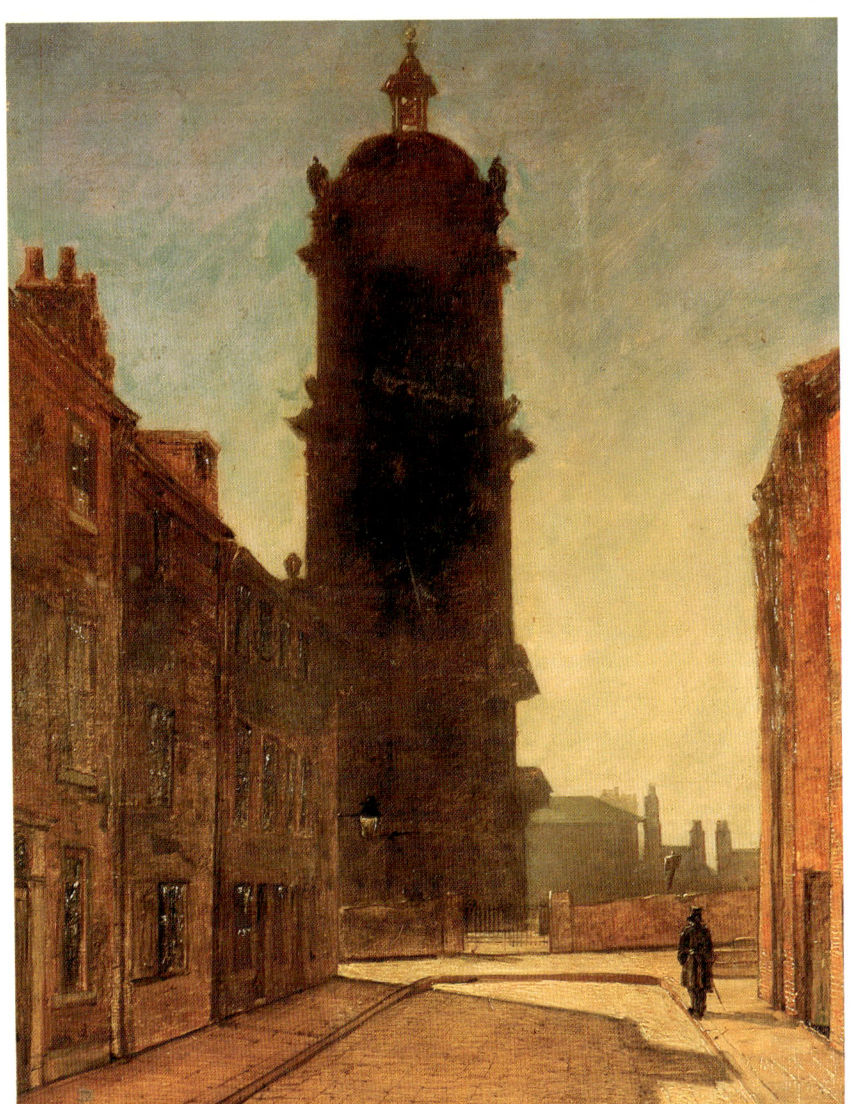

There were quiet corners, places where the hustle and bustle could be forgotten and where life moved at a gentler pace. Cheney Square near St. Paul's Church, now the area of the Peace Gardens, was appropriately quiet, as was Watson Walk where people could sit down in the oyster bar and take the weight off their feet.

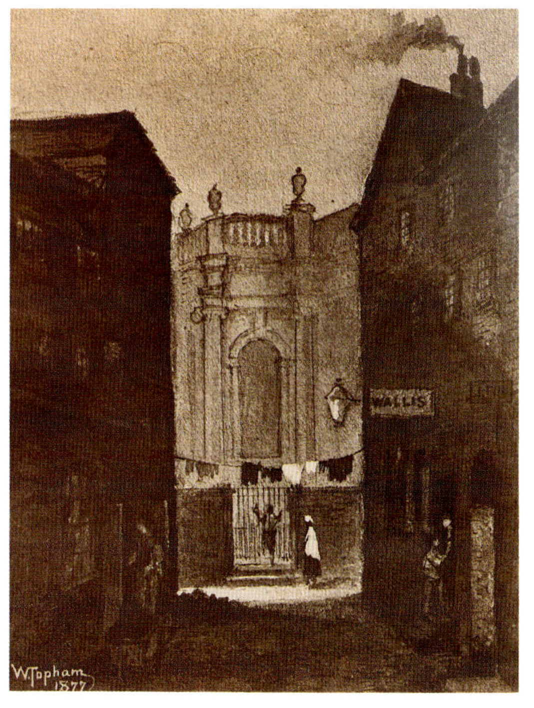

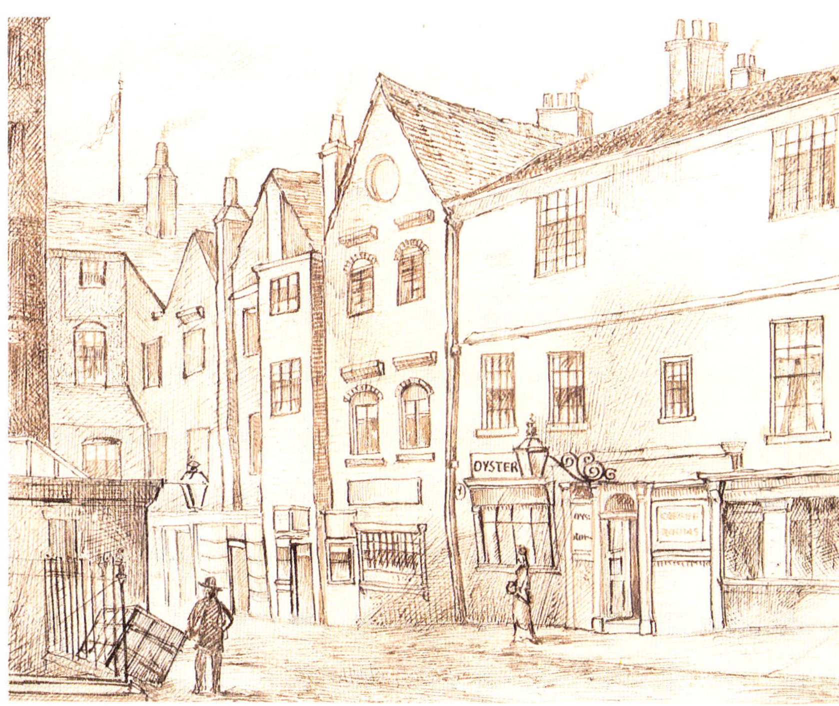

Above left

W. *Topham*
Cabbage Alley 1877

W. *Topham*
In Watson Walk 1883

W. *Topham*
*Silver Street Head c.*1880

THE *Outskirts*

Not far from the town centre the pace of life changed dramatically. One never had far to go to make contact with the traditional steadiness of life on the fringes of Sheffield. It is, perhaps, hard for us to believe that 100 years ago Hunter's Bar, now marooned on a traffic island, was a rural outpost on the turnpike road, and that cottages at Highfields, now the site of the library, by the fork in the road to Heeley and Abbeydale, were a haven of country life. The windswept and lonely ruins of Sheffield Manor were reached by a potholed lane, whilst the tranquillity of Vulcan Dam at the bottom of Ellin Street, near St Mary's and Bramall Lane, is now buried beneath the ring road and a brown brick pyramidal office block.

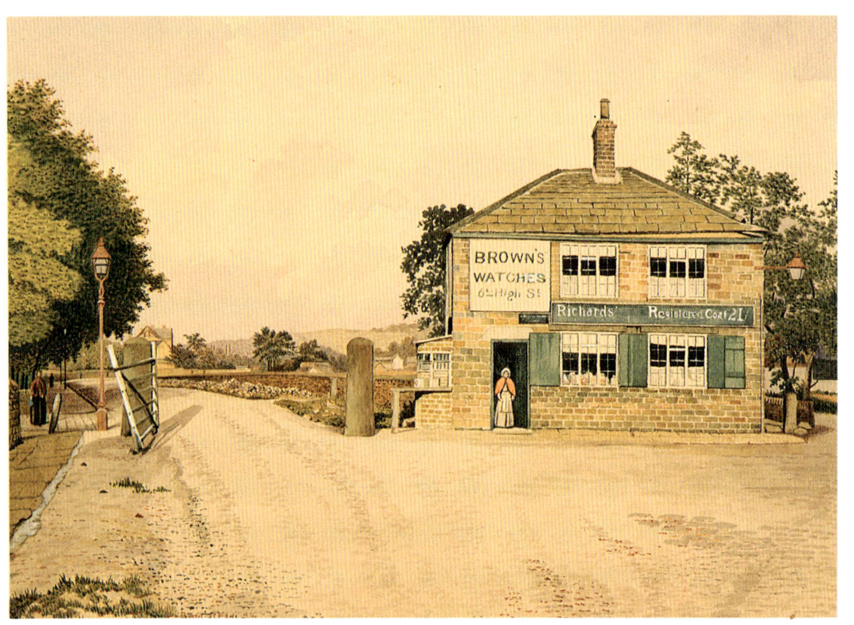

S. Bell
Hunter's Bar c.1870

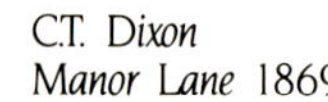

C.T. Dixon
Manor Lane 1869

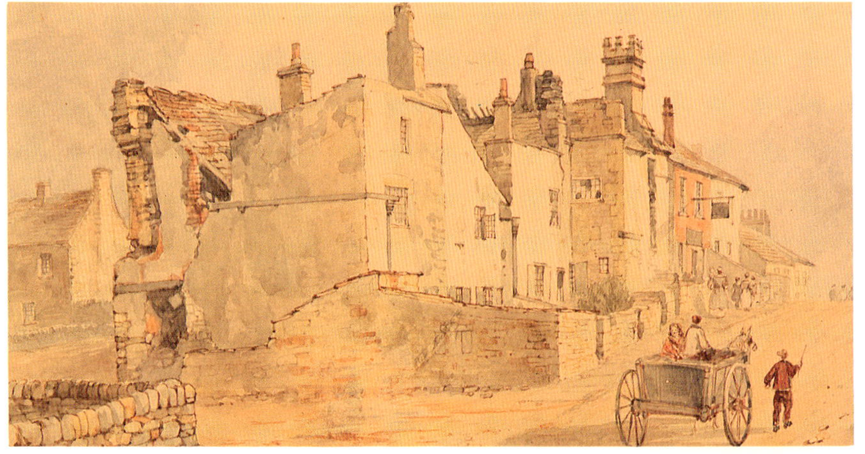

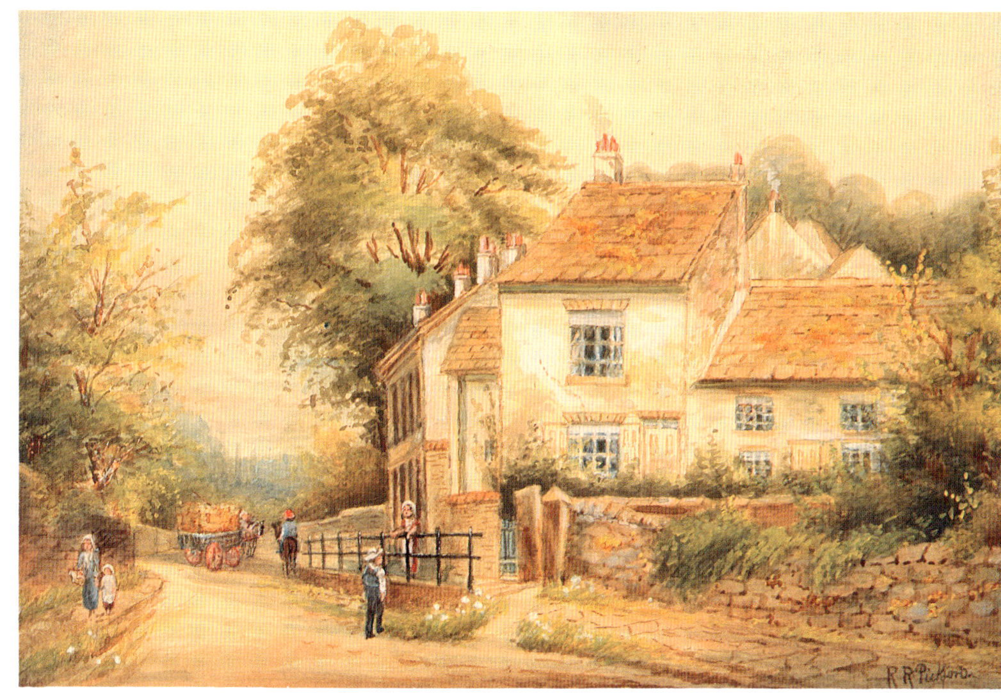

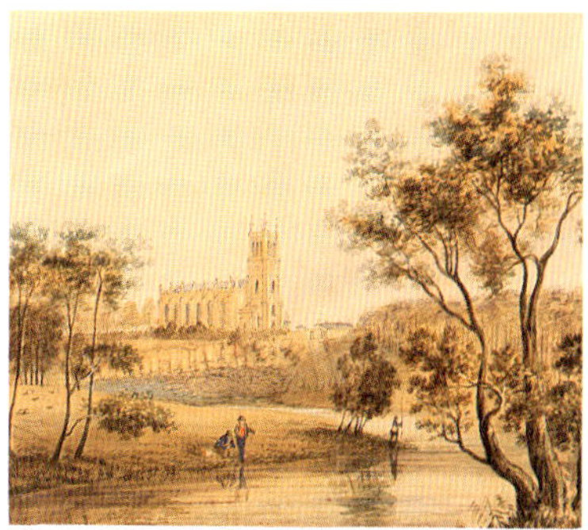

I. Shaw
Christ Church, Attercliffe
c. 1845

R.R. Pickford
*Highfields c.*1879

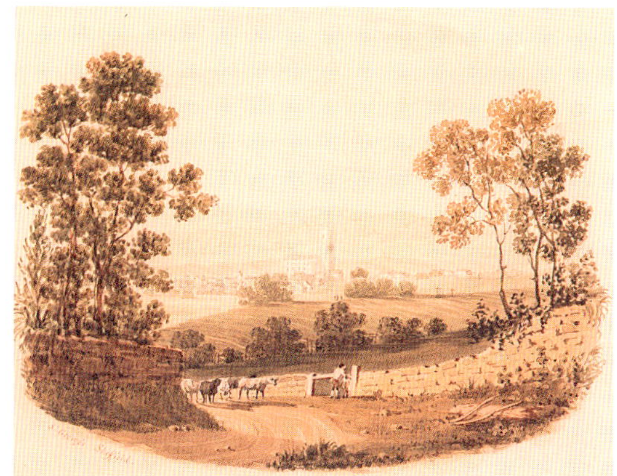

W. Lowe
St. Georges Church, Sheffield *c.*1830

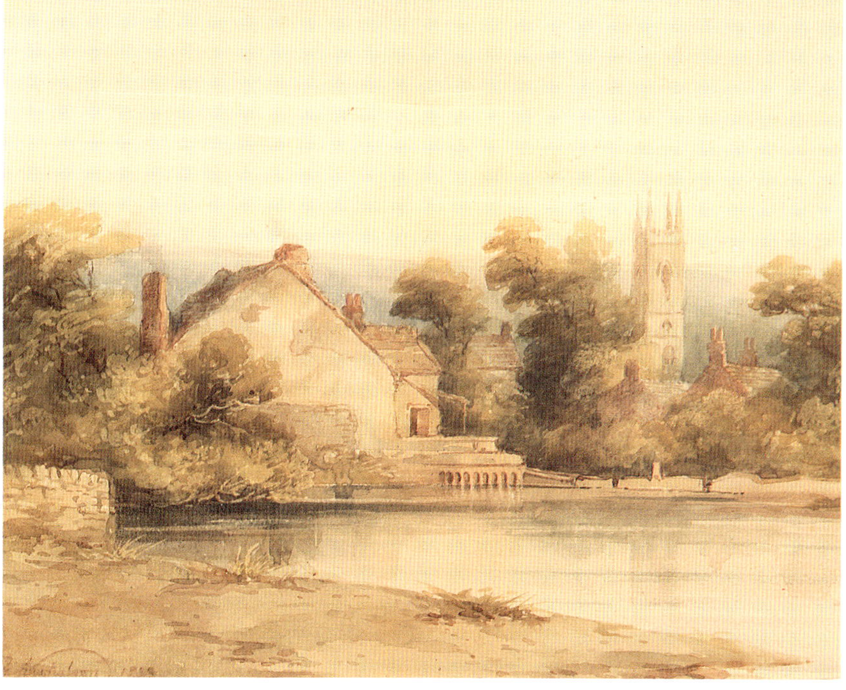

G. Nicholson
Vulcan Dam and Ellin Street 1833

Regency SHEFFIELD

E. Bennett
Carver Street Methodist Chapel 1807

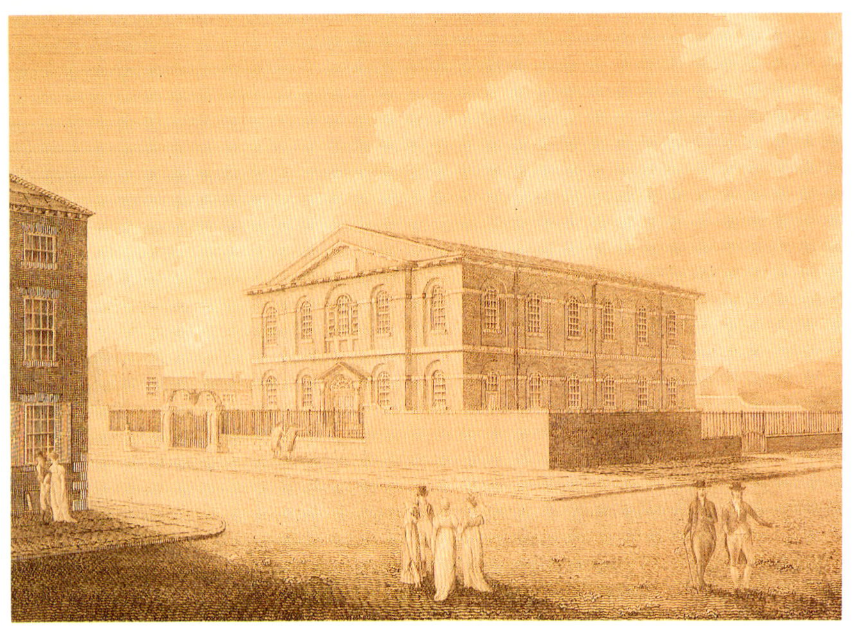

An impression of a refined, middle-class, leisured Sheffield is portrayed by those artists keen to record views of new buildings. The elegance of the Georgian and Regency period is splendidly captured in studies of Carver Street Methodist Chapel, still there fronting West Street, and the Royal Infirmary, now stranded between a cheap and cheerful post-modern supermarket and the gaunt, grey and spiritless Kelvin Flats. Both buildings are presented as fine, graceful additions to the town, peopled with equally elegant and fashionable figures, at a time when Old Sheffield Plate products, particularly candlesticks in the refined Neo-Classical style, were being exported from the town to grace the homes of the wealthy all over the country.

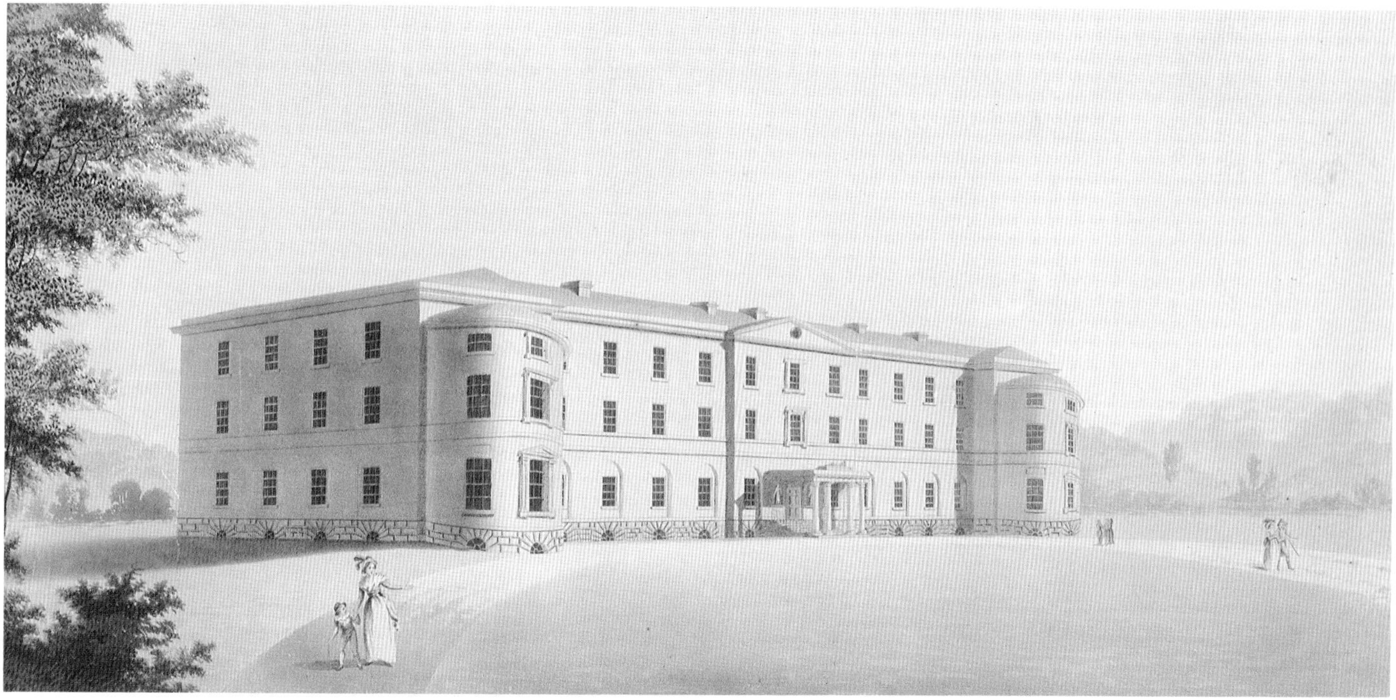

J. Rawsthorne
Sheffield Royal Infirmary 1804

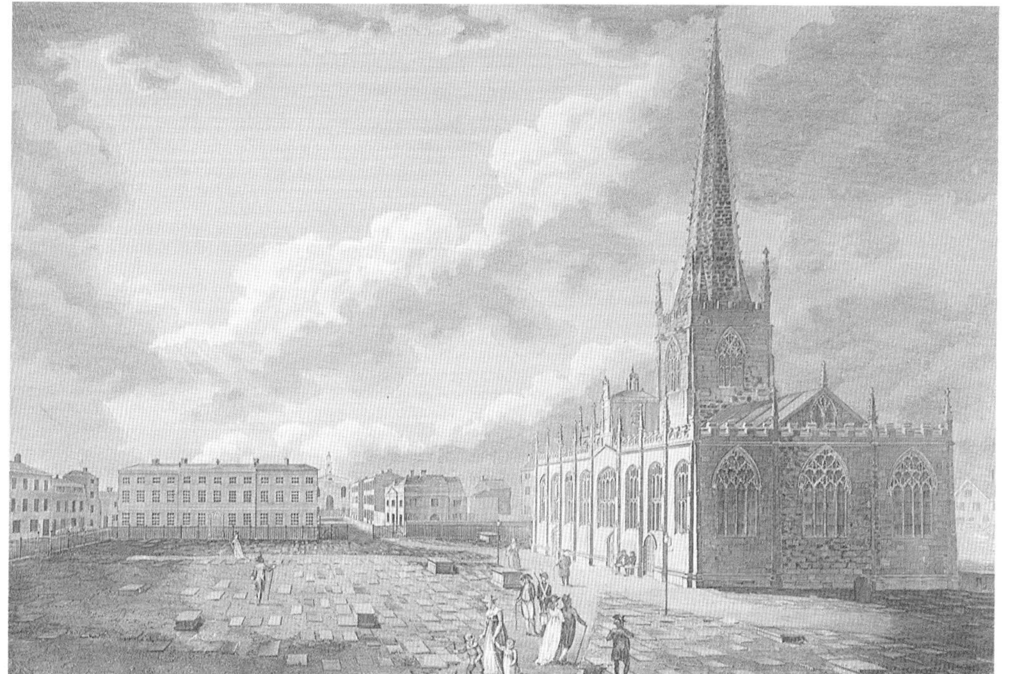

T. Harris
The Parish Church 1793

Victorian

RESPECTABILIT

I. Shaw
Botanical Gardens c. 1850

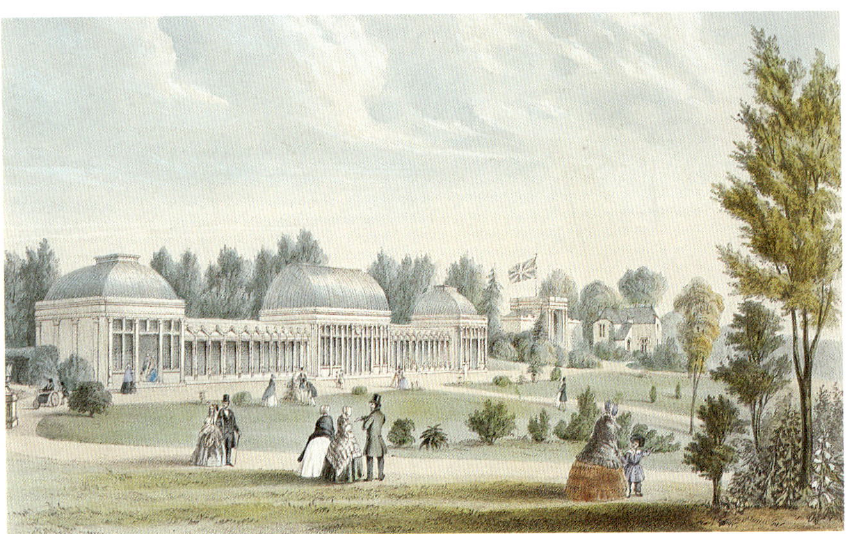

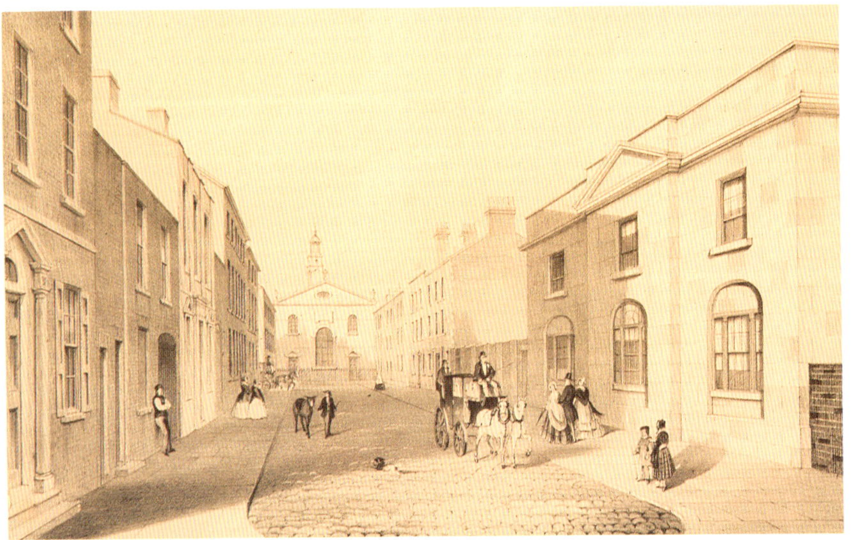

The same treatment of linking new buildings with the well-to-do society which frequented them, is evident in the work of several mid-Victorian artists. In particular, Isaac Shaw presents the brand new Botanical Gardens, St James' Church and St Stephen's Church as smart new spots to see and in which to be seen. All the characters peopling these scenes appear virtuous and godly, immaculately dressed with not a hair out of place. It was Sheffield as it could be, as it might be in certain places, on Sundays. It was not Sheffield as it really was, for most people. After all, where were the ordinary people? Where were the ordinary buildings, the homes of the ordinary people? The answer is that there was no room for ordinary people and simple buildings in the middle of town in these 19th century views of prosperity and progress. Arthur White proudly records the demolition of old Sheffield at the top of High Street as vernacular buildings are pulled down at night to widen the street and to expose the full glory of High Victorian Gothick architecture, watched by smartly dressed people, of course.

I. Shaw
St. James' Church c.1850

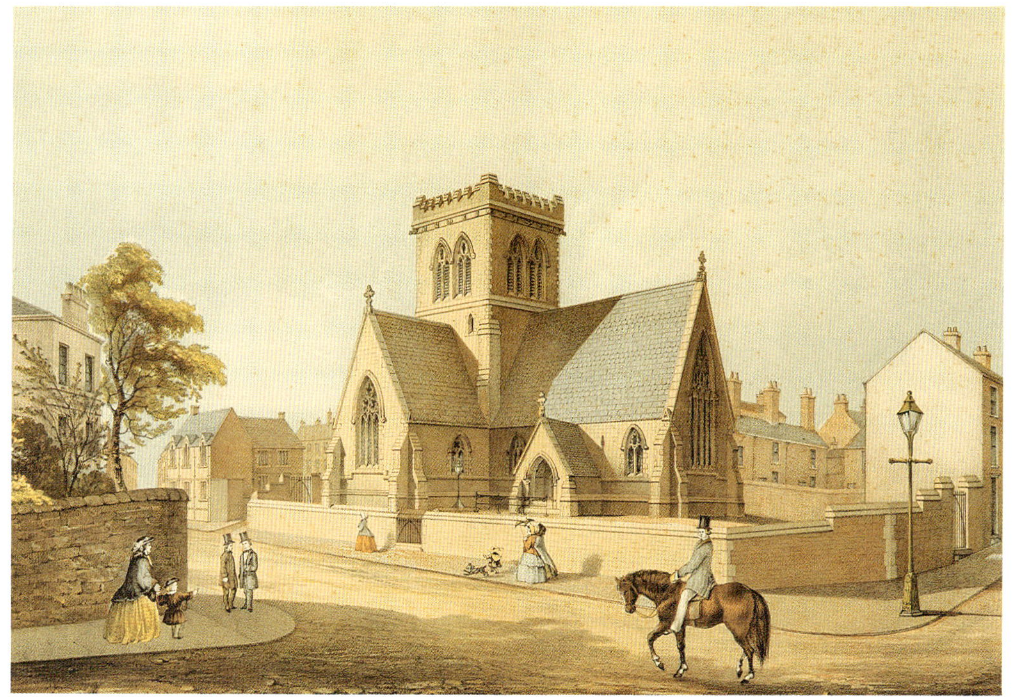

E. Hides
St. Stephen's Church c.1860

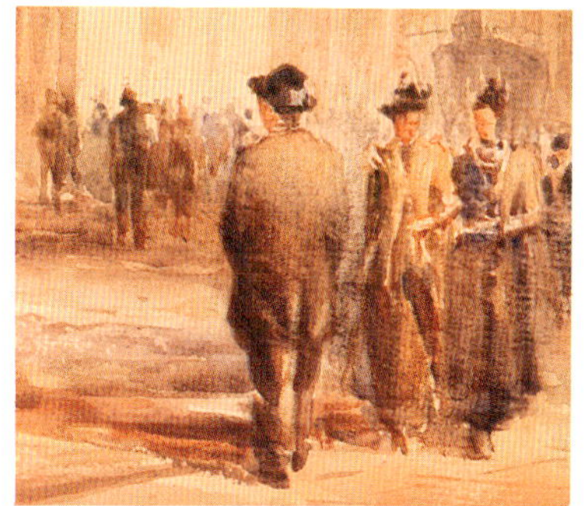

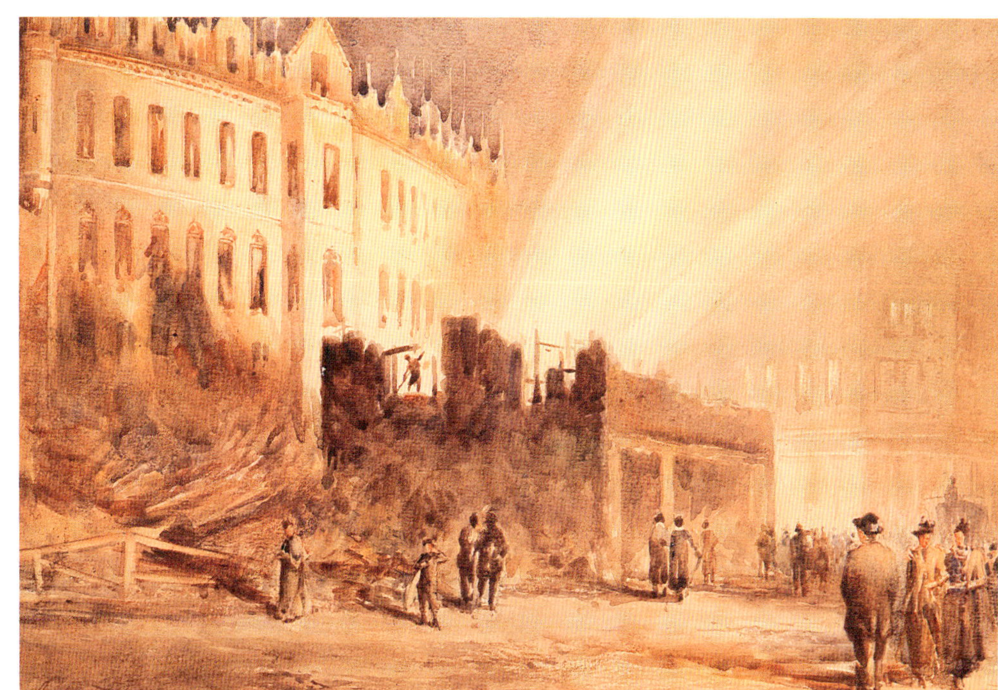

A. White
High Street 1896

COMMON *People*

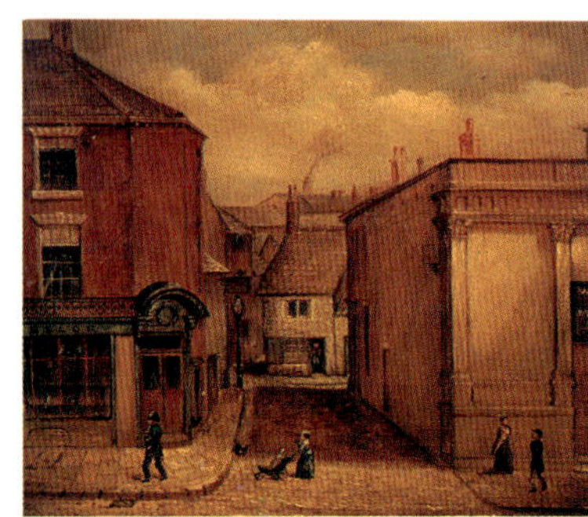

T. Aldam
Balm Green 1858

Fortunately, not all artists worked with the same intention in recording fine buildings, and it is possible to reach a balanced view of Sheffield in the 19th century by looking at the work of those artists who chose to set fine buildings as background to incident in the lives of ordinary people. Edward Blore left a remarkable series of engravings, amongst which his views of St Paul's Church featuring a woman sitting on a step with her baby is surpassed only by his close observation of St Peter's, the parish church. In this, he chooses to add human interest by showing the pot-seller unpacking and spreading her wares out along the pavement, whilst a boy swings on the churchyard railings alongside. The same concern to bring imposing buildings into focus by their contact with everyday life is evident in the work of Alwyn Holland whose night-time view of St Paul's is memorable for its street scene with the hot-chestnut man beneath the gas lamp.

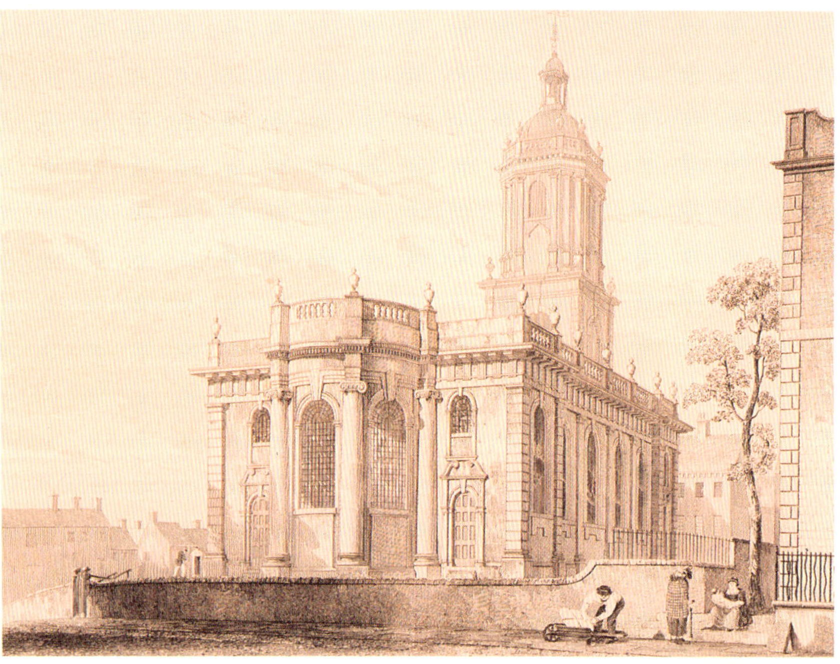

E. *Blore*
St. Pauls Church 1819

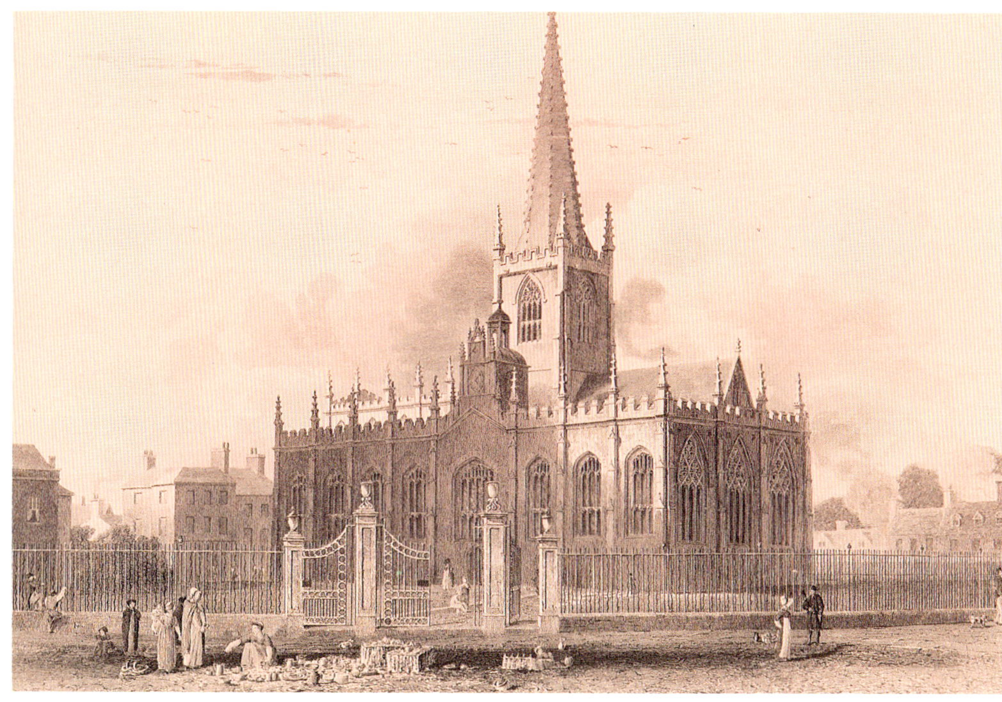

E. Blore
St. Peter's Church 1819

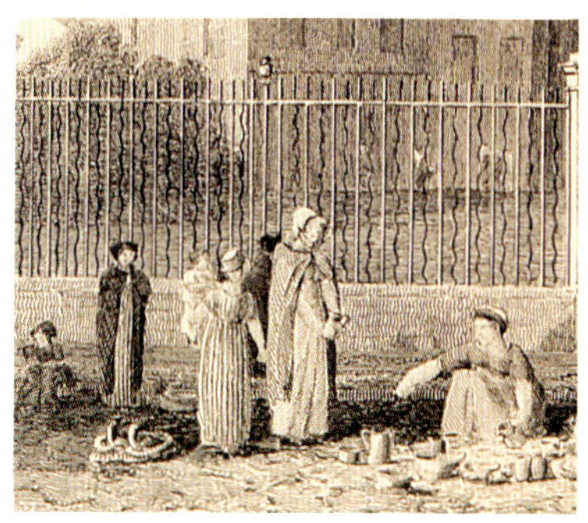

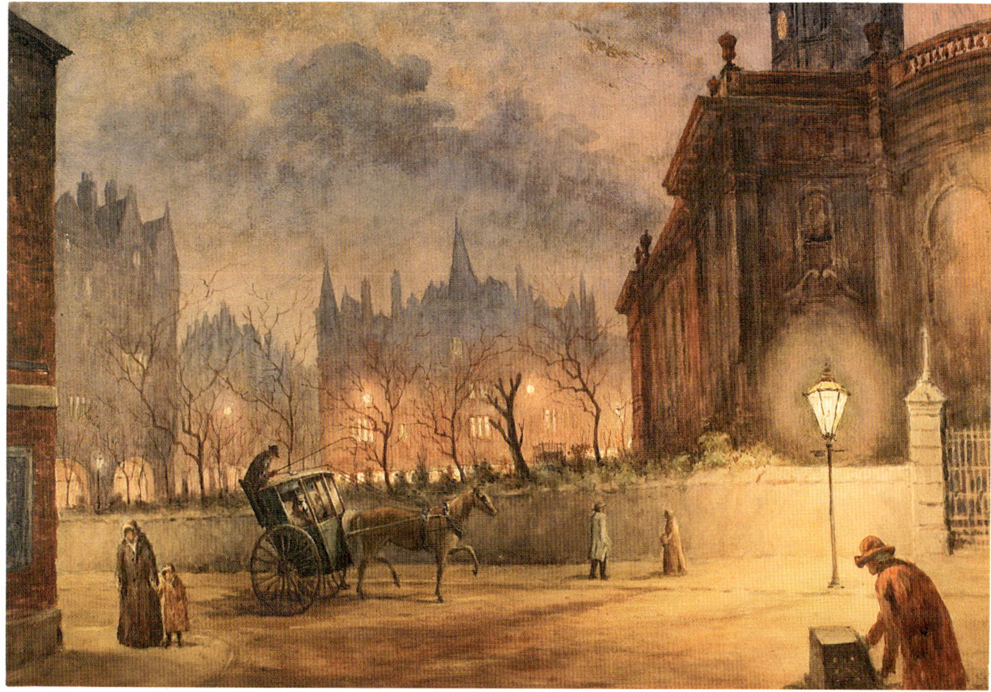

A. Holland
St. Paul's churchyard 1910

Everyday LIFE

A desire to portray scenes of everyday life in Sheffield coupled with an evident ambition to record quaint and picturesque corners of town is best exemplified in the paintings of Arthur Wilson. His chocolate-box cover pictures vividly bring to life moments closely observed in Hartshead or along Trippet Lane, where children play, run errands, or are obliged to earn a few pence selling newspapers. The old dilapidated houses down Snig Hill, with people busy doing their shopping are scenes of activity frozen in time.

A. Wilson
Hartshead 1895

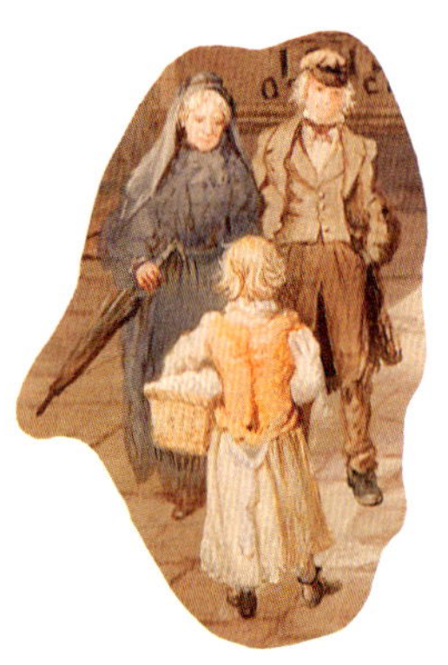

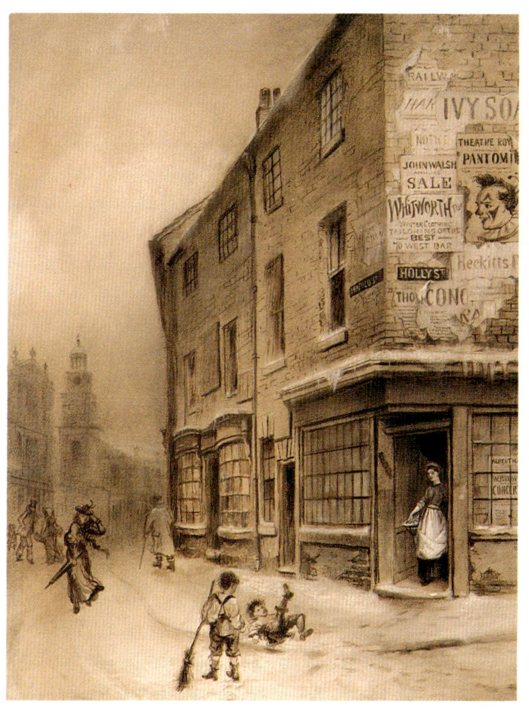

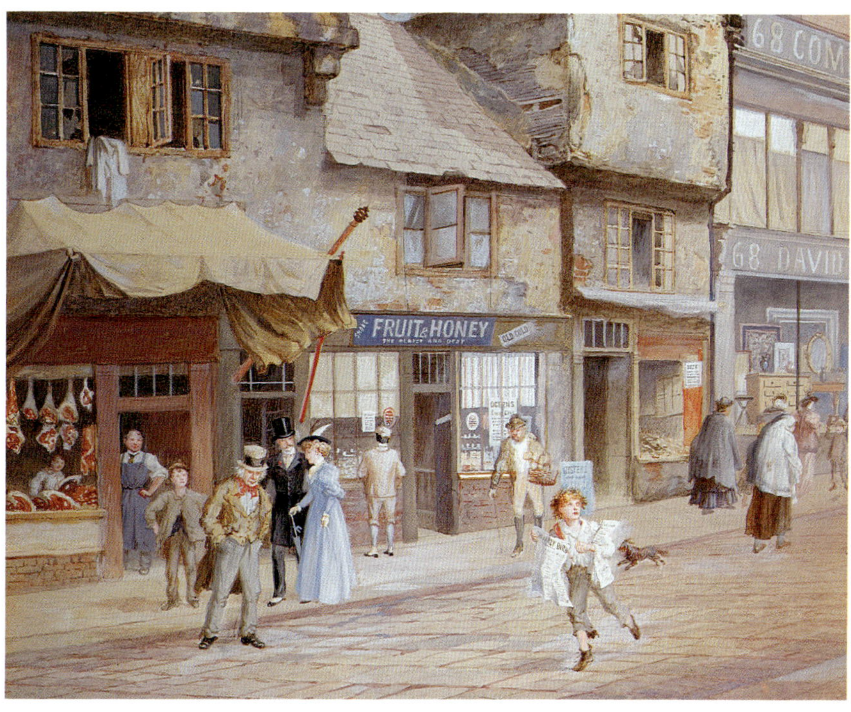

A. Wilson
Snig Hill 1895

Above left

A. Wilson
Corner of Pinfold Street and Holly Street
1895

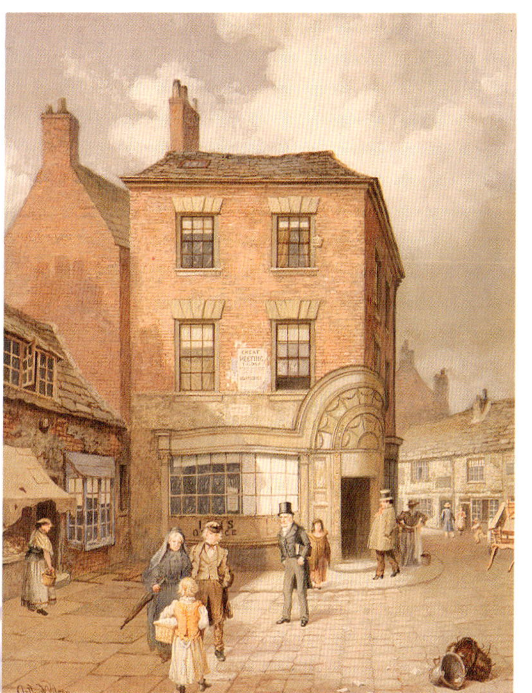

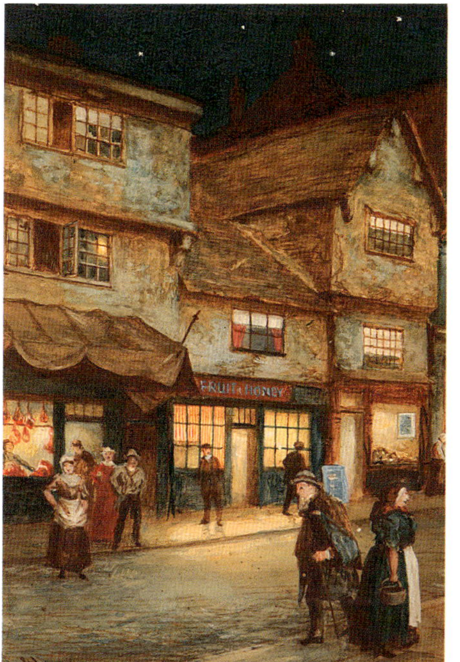

A. Wilson
Snig Hill at night 1895

Far left

A. Wilson
Iris Office 1895

W. Boden
Steps in Pond Street, Sheffield 1903

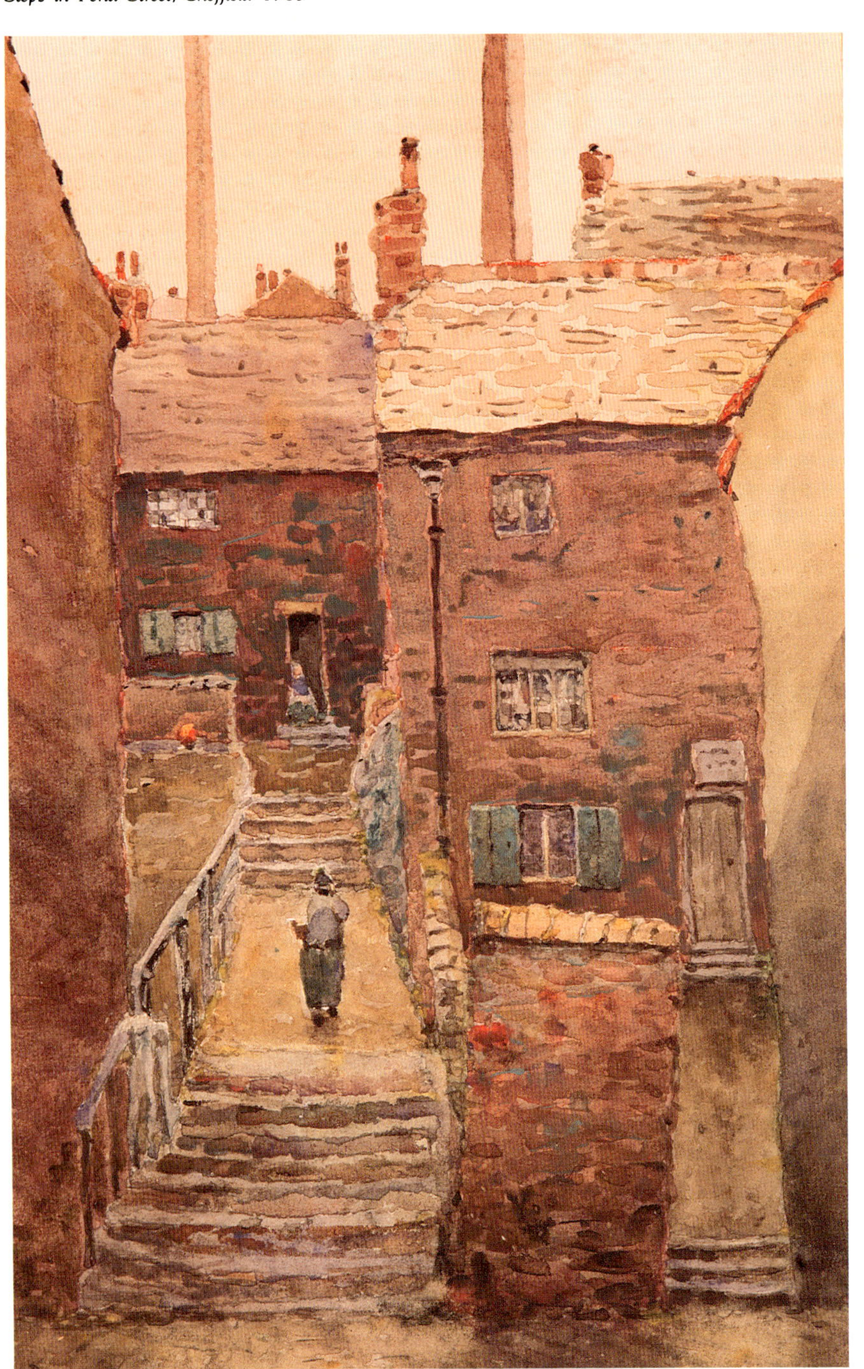

TOWN
Houses

People's homes in the heart of Sheffield can occasionally be glimpsed in views of other buildings, but W. Topham, a prolific painter of small post-card-sized pictures, seems to have made it his job to paint virtually every old building, corner and alley in the town, thus leaving us a permanent record of where people lived. His view of old houses on Balm Green, where the City Hall now stands, was also painted by Thomas Aldam, showing how the houses were tucked away behind the Weights and Measures Office, which fronted the main street. Streets of terraced houses, lit by the occasional gas lamp, stretched out along Pond Street and behind the Midland Station up Park Hill, where houses seemed to be stacked almost on top of one another. They were approached by long flights of stone steps and Bernard Street steps in the Park was a particularly hard climb, especially with bags of shopping. Down Cambridge Street, where a whole family might have to share one room of a house, living conditions were cramped and unhealthy. For many people, poverty was a real fact of life, especially in the back to back houses and courts in the town centre. This, the desperate plight of poor people, is portrayed with humanity by Alwyn Holland in his picture of Croft Hall and Porridge Row.

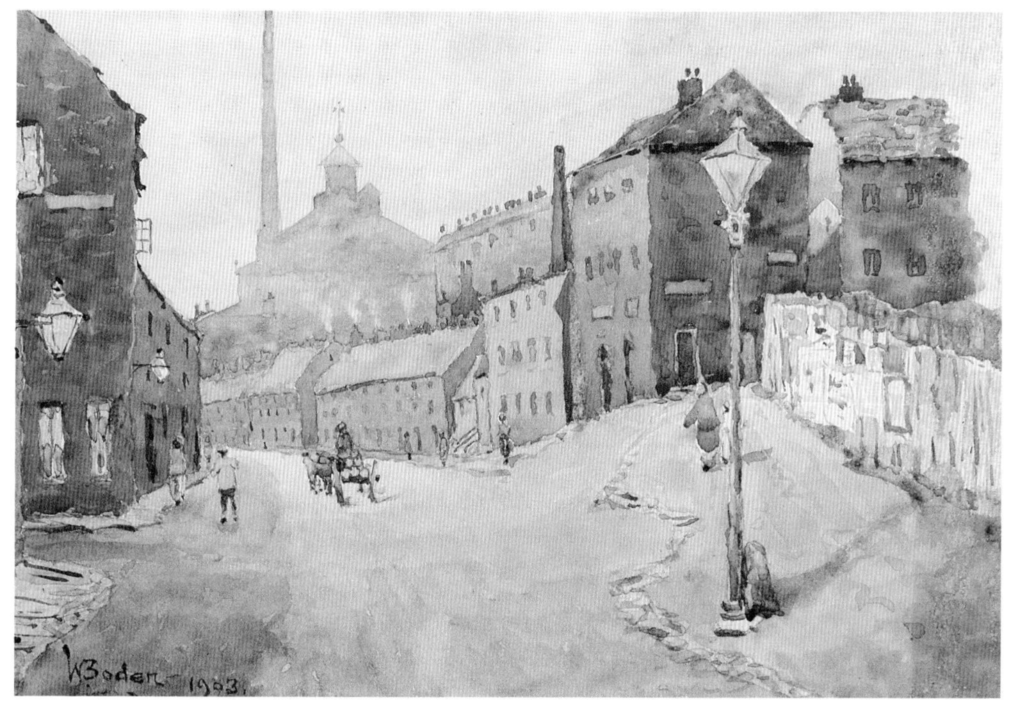

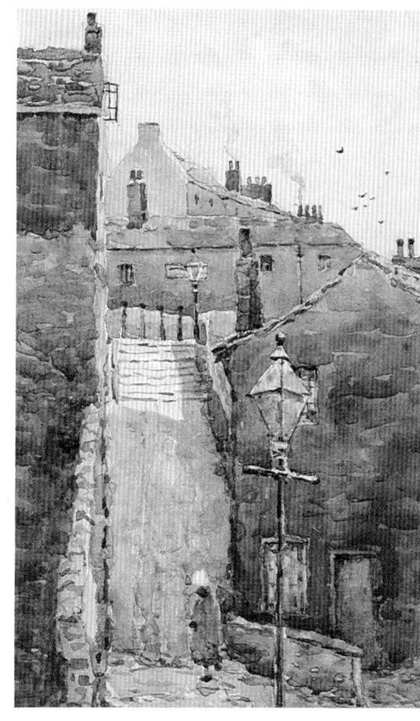

W. Boden
View in the Park, Sheffield 1903

A. Holland
*Croft Hall and Porridge Row c.*1910

Above W. Boden
Pond Street 1903

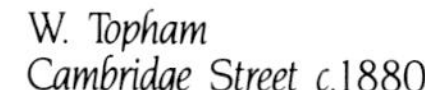

W. Topham
*Cambridge Street c.*1880

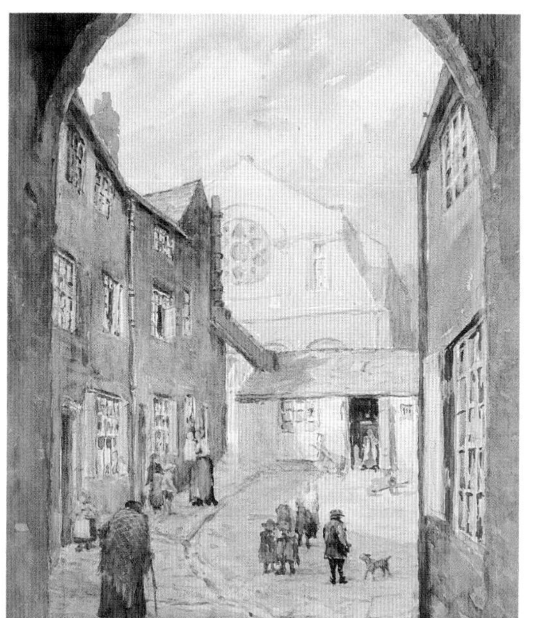

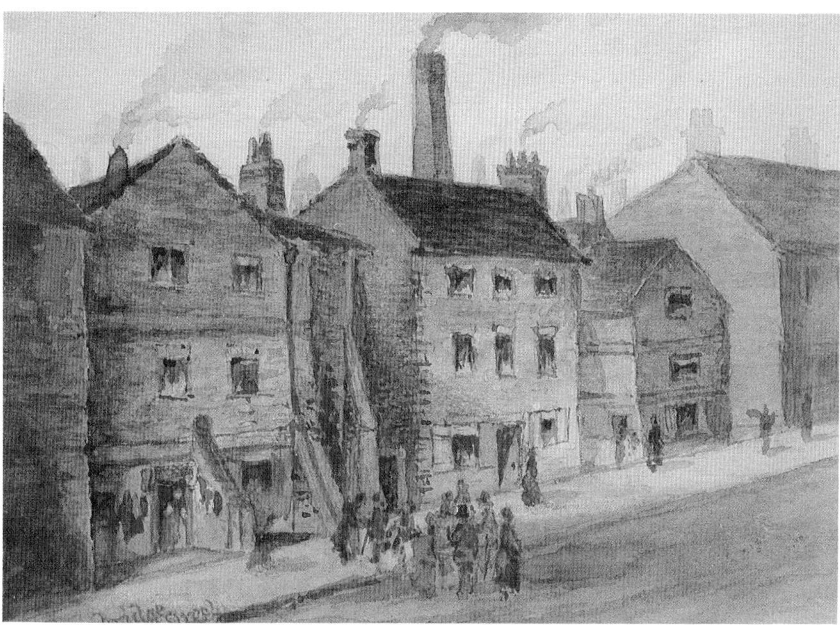

THE *Road* TO WORK

G. Sykes
St. Paul's Church from Union Street 1858

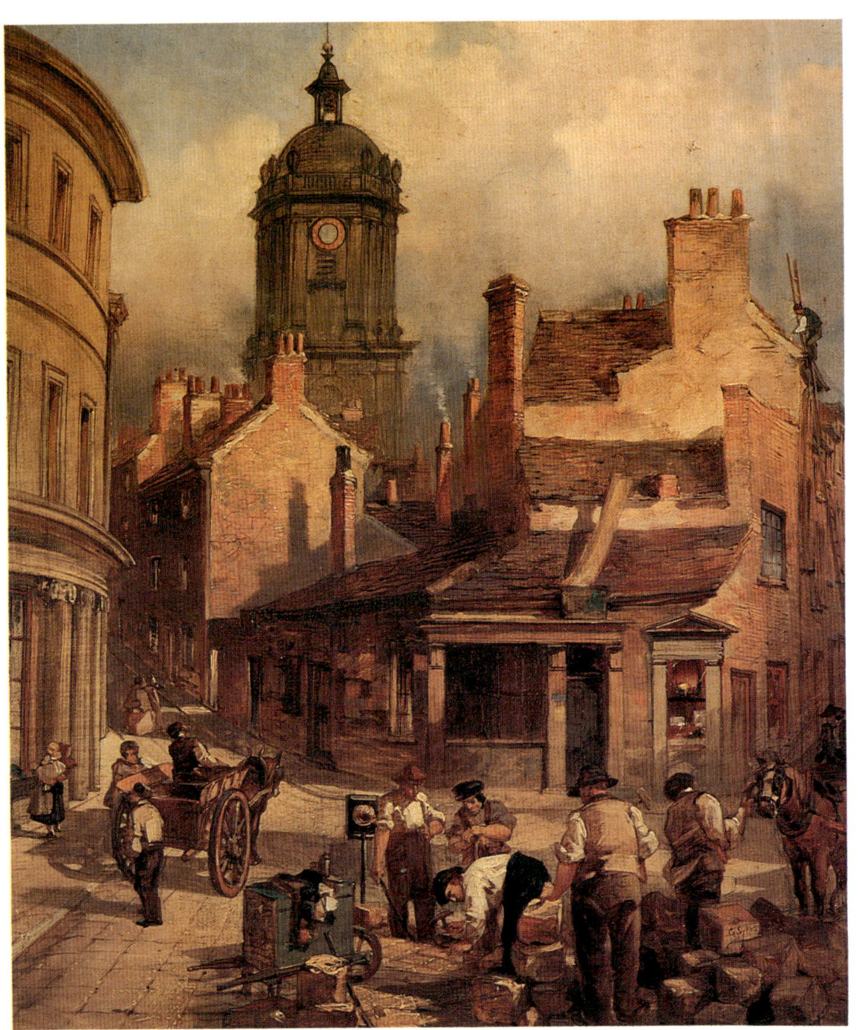

A feeling for the dignity of working people comes across in William Keeling's early morning view of Trippet Lane, where women wrapped in shawls are trudging along the road to workshop and factory. This is the way of life for most people, and the same quality of respect for the daily labours of ordinary folk is evident in Godfrey Sykes' view of St Paul's Church and Union Street, where a gang of road menders are busy about their work laying setts.

A very different view of working life is, however, presented in an anonymous painting of Sheffield from Lady's Bridge in 1875. Individual human endeavour is ignored: rather, a mass of people swarms over Lady's Bridge at the end of the working day, escaping from the soot-blackened factories and smoke-belching chimneys. The human spirit is crushed by its soulless surroundings and boring routine.

H.H. Earl
Lady's Bridge 1844

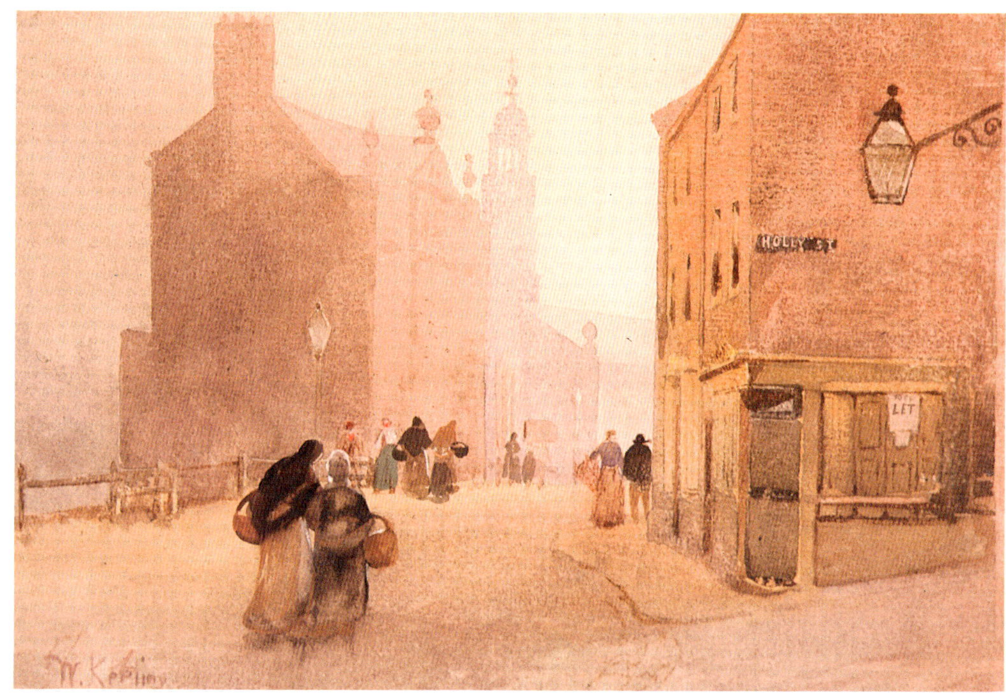

W. Keeling
Early morn on Trippet Lane c.1885

Anonymous
Sheffield from Lady's Bridge 1875

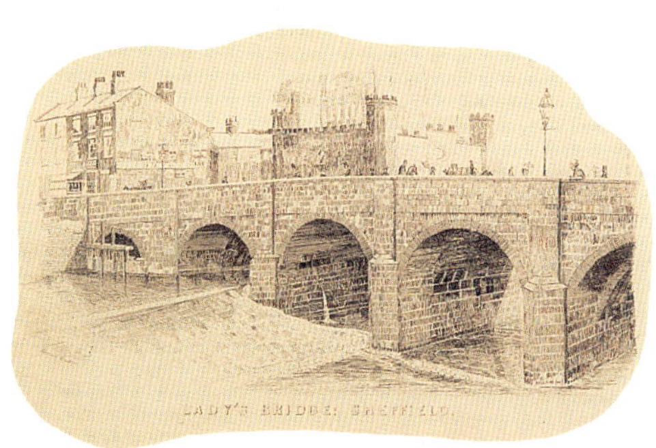

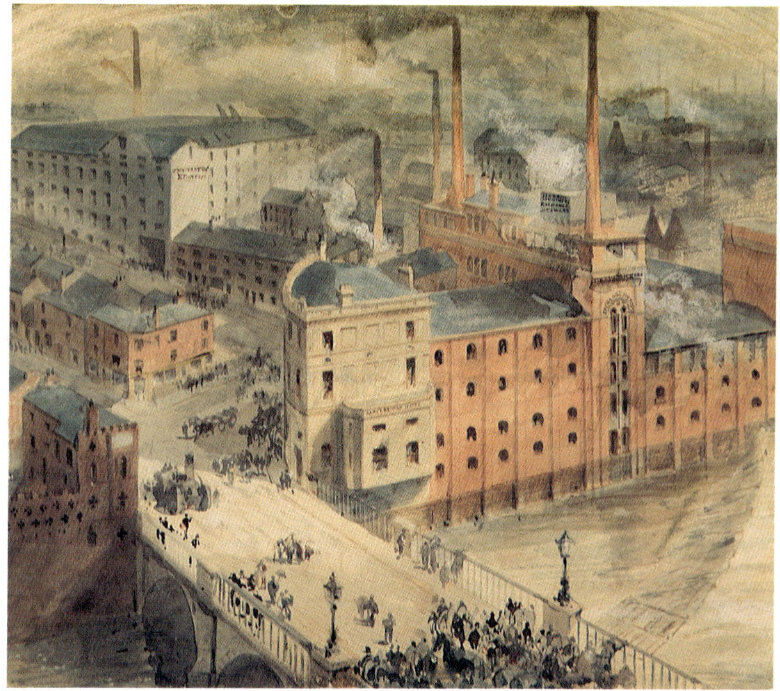

Smoky SHEFFIELD

By the end of the 19th century the growth of industry in Sheffield had resulted in levels of atmospheric pollution inconceivable today. Choking smoke lay like a blanket over the town as shown in Alwyn Holland's **Sheffield from above the Midland Station** and Joseph Pennell's view from the River Don. Fog, smog, coughs, bronchitis had become an accepted part of life, and death.

J. Pennell
Fog, steam and smoke on the River Don c.1909

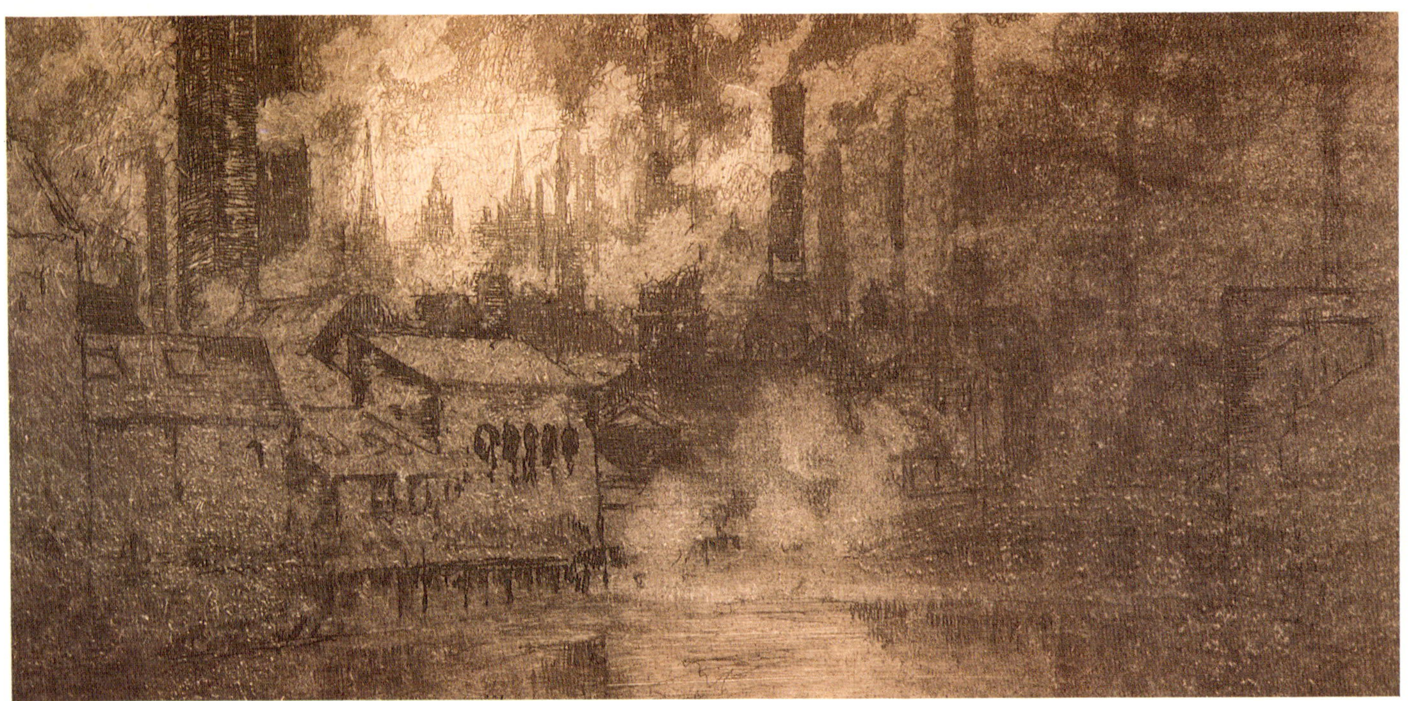

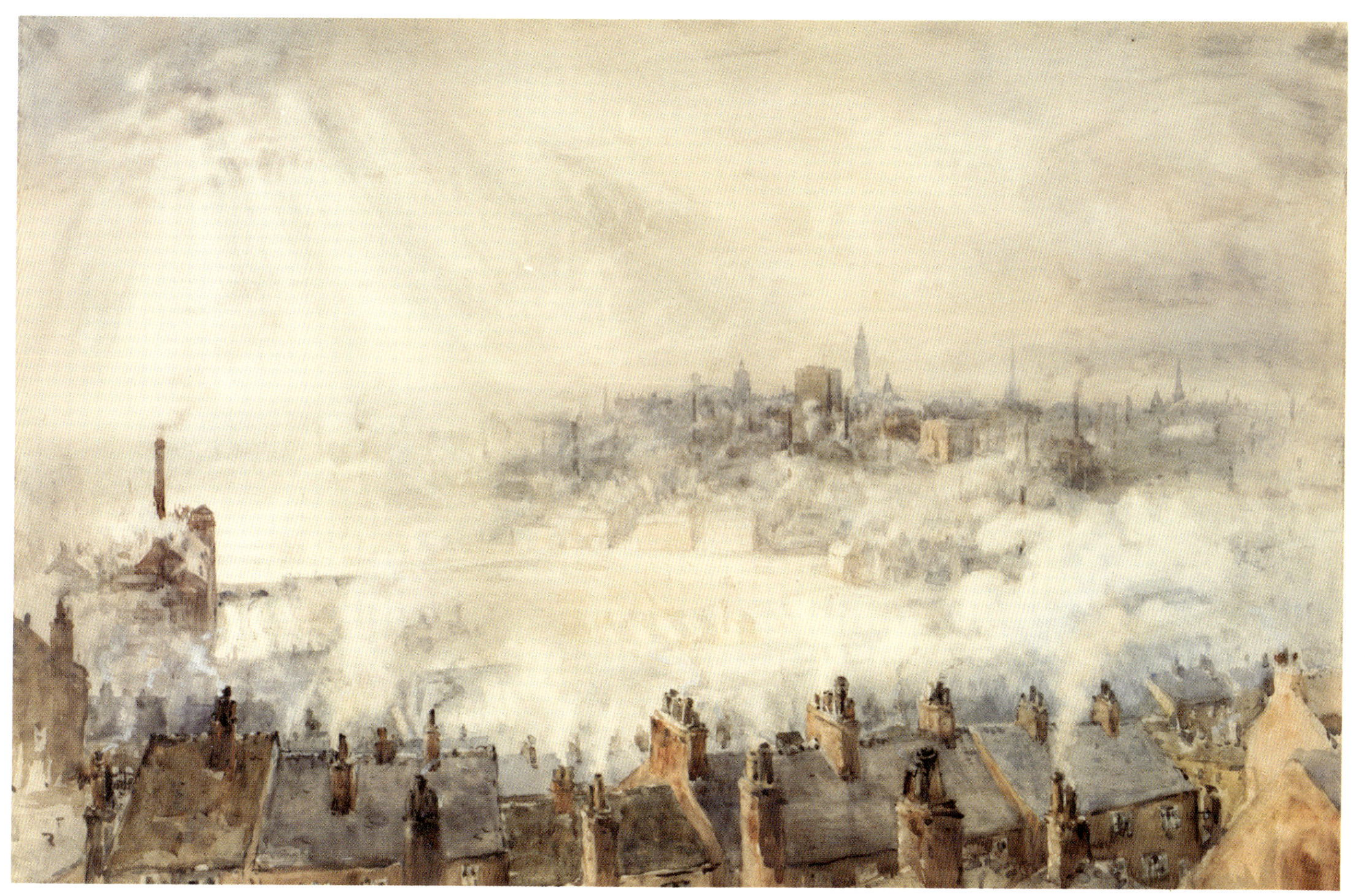

A. Holland
Sheffield from above the Midland Station 1909

Fresh Air

PARKS & COUNTRYSIDE

But there were windy days which whisked the smoke away, and it was always easy on Sundays to find fresh air at Crookesmoor or in the Rivelin Valley. Weston Park was not far away from town and a delightful walk could still be had from the Canal Basin along the towpath to the green pastures at Tinsley.

W. Boden
Sheffield Canal Basin 1902

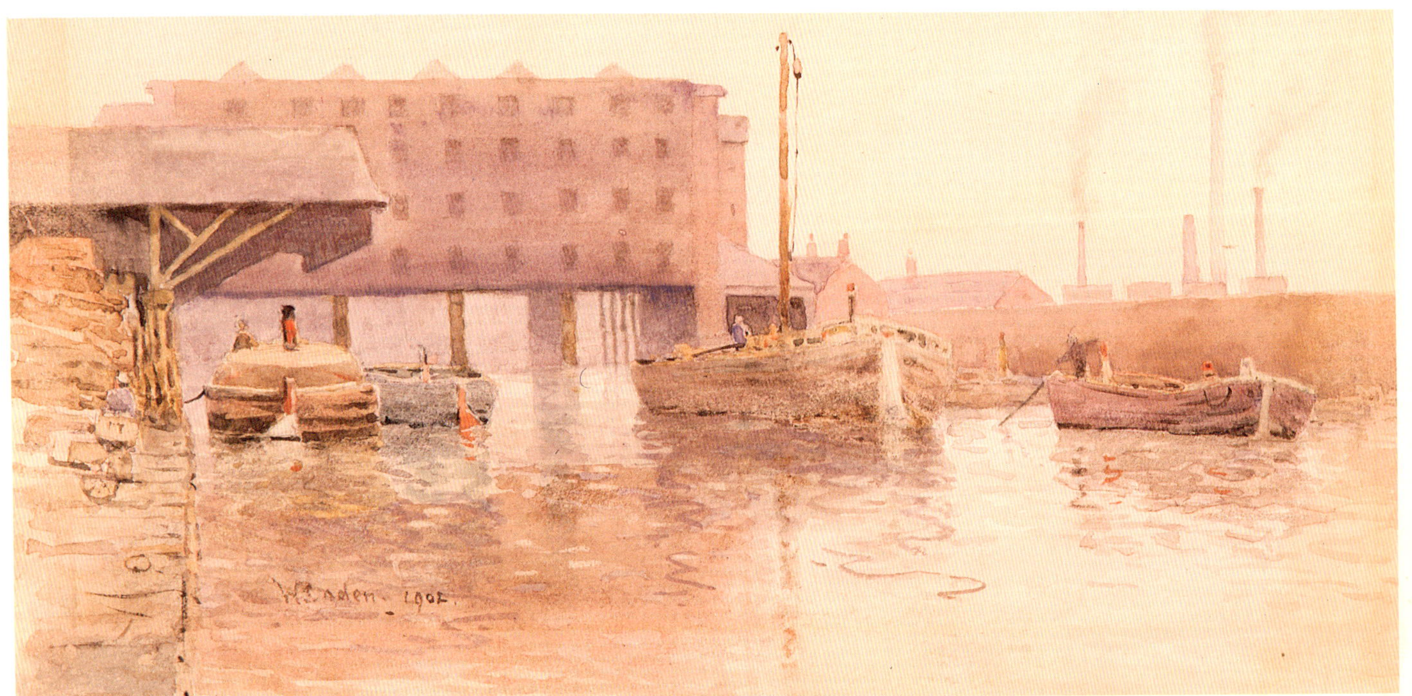

A. Wilson
Weston Park c1910

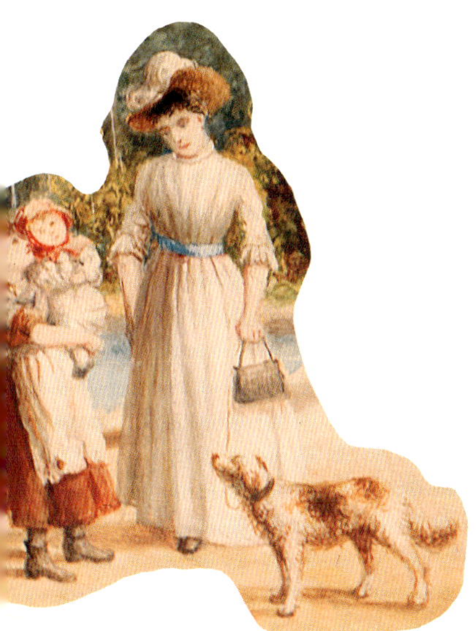

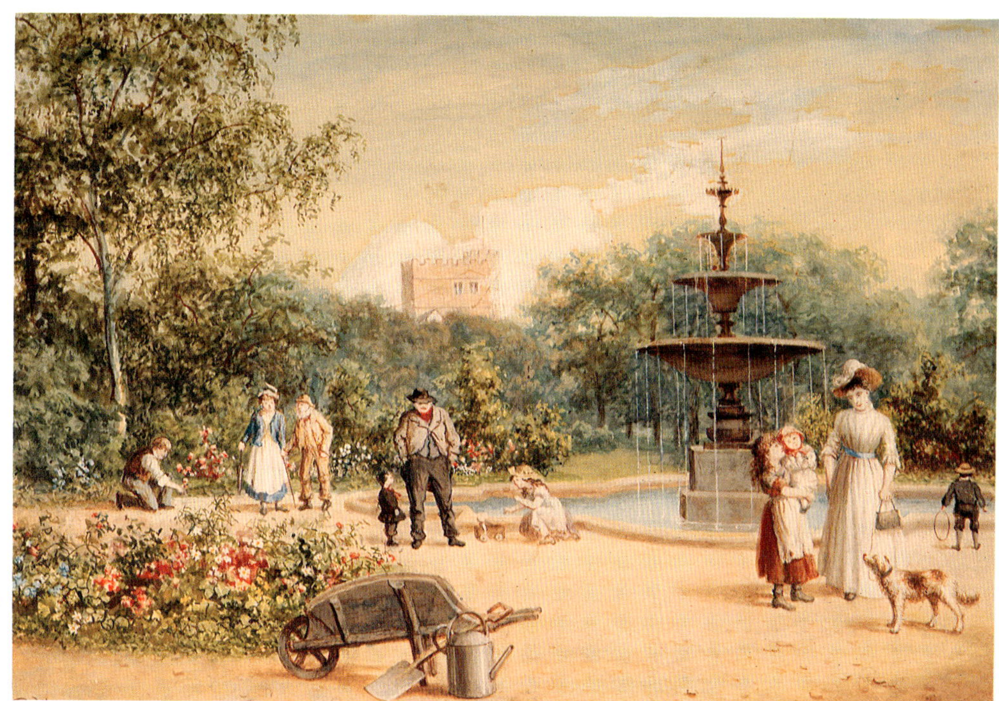

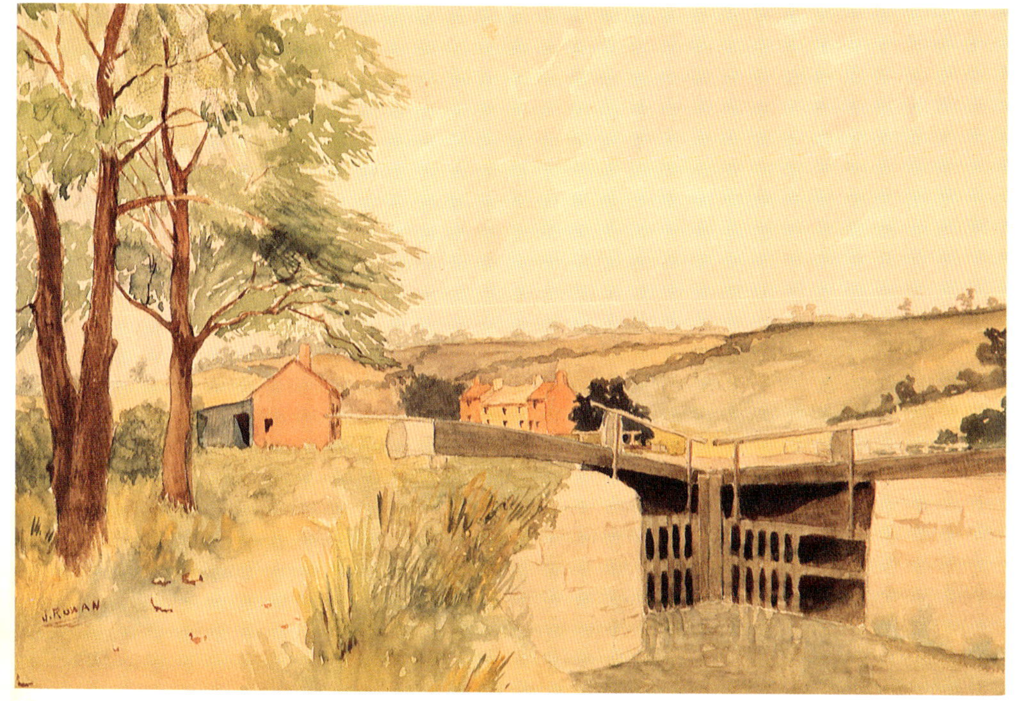

J. Rowan
Tinsley Lock c.1890

All the paintings used as illustrations in this booklet, with the exception of T. Nisbet **Waingate** (1837) featured by courtesy of Sheffield City Art Galleries and A. Wilson **Snig Hill** (1895) which is privately owned, are from the local paintings collection of Sheffield City Museums.